ys to Pay

Less Tax

Perfectly Legal Ways to Pay Less Tax

140 tips that will save you money

Sara Williams

PEARSON

Harlow, England • London • New York • Boston • San Francisco • Toronto • Sydney
Auckland • Singapore • Hong Kong • Tokyo • Seoul • Taipei • New Delhi
Cape Town • São Paulo • Mexico City • Madrid • Amsterdam • Munich • Paris • Milan

PEARSON EDUCATION LIMITED

Edinburgh Gate
Harlow CM20 2JE
Tel: +44 (0)1279 623623
Fax: +44 (0)1279 431059
Website: www.pearson.com/uk

First published in Great Britain in 2012
© Vitesse Media Plc 2012

Pearson Education is not responsible for the content of third-party internet sites.

ISBN: 978-1-4479-2947-5

British Library Cataloguing-in-Publication Data
A catalogue record for this book is available from the British Library

Library of Congress Cataloging-in-Publication Data
A catalog record for this book is available from the Library of Congress

10 9 8 7 6 5 4 3 2 1
16 15 14 13 12

Typeset in 9.5/13pt Apex by 30
Printed in Great Britain by Henry Ling Ltd, at the Dorset Press, Dorchester, Dorset

Contents

Preface vii
About the author ix
Introduction x

1 An overview of income tax: what it is, what it means to you and how to pay it 1

2 Make the most of what you earn: these things are all free of tax 9

3 How you can pay less tax and how to get it back if you've paid too much 17

4 What if you have tax problems? Solutions for dealing with them 39

5 Tax and your home 49

6 Savings, investments and pensions. How to make the most of putting money away 65

7 Making the most of fringe benefits and minimising capital gains tax 75

8 Gifts and passing your money on (but not to the tax man) 87

9 How to save money when filling in your tax return 95

10 Useful leaflets, forms and contacts 121

Index 130

Preface

No one likes to pay tax, but most of us recognise that there are important reasons why we need to pay it. But what many of us don't realise is that many people pay more tax than they need to. This money legally belongs to you and you're fully entitled to ask for it back, or even better, not pay it in the first place.

In recent months there have been lots of stories in the news about tax evasion and the things that the government is planning to do to crack down on the unlawful non-payment of tax. But please do remember that whilst tax evasion is illegal, ensuring that you've not paid too much tax is well within the law and *Perfectly Legal Ways to Pay Less Tax* will help you save money without getting into trouble with the tax authorities. Whether it's making sure that you've got your tax code right, through to not overpaying on national insurance, making the most of ISAs and pensions or claiming the right amount of tax credits, we're providing 140 above-board methods of saving money by paying as little tax as legally possible, or claiming back money that you have overpaid.

Sara Williams, 2012

Note

The publisher and the author have made strenuous efforts to check the accuracy of the information in this book. If by chance a mistake or omission has occurred, we are sorry and neither the author or the publisher are able to take responsibility if you suffer any loss or problem as a result of it. But if you have any suggestions about how we can improve the content of this book then please write to Sara Williams, *Perfectly Legal Ways to Pay Less Tax*, Vitesse Media, Octavia House, 50 Banner Street, London EC1Y 8ST.

About the author

Sara Williams is a former investment analyst and financial journalist. She has contributed many articles on tax and finance to national newspapers and for a number of years wrote for *Which?*, including the *Which? Tax-Saving Guide* and the *Which? Book of Tax*. She is also the author of the *Financial Times Guide to Business Start Up*. Sara is now the executive chair of AIM-listed Vitesse Media plc, which offers research, digital and social media, and event management in the tax, business and investment areas. She holds qualifications in investment advice and management.

Introduction

The taxes you might pay

There are several ways in which the government raises money from taxpayers. Some of the taxes are as follows:

- income tax – some of your income is taxed at varying rates
- capital gains tax – some of the gains you make on investments or possessions may be taxed at varying rates
- inheritance tax – when you die, some of the money you leave to others could be taxed, and some lifetime gifts are taxable too
- pre-owned assets tax – an income tax on the benefit you are deemed to get if you still use or enjoy something you have given away
- national insurance – this is compulsory only for people who are earning: employees and their employers, the self-employed or business partners.

Other taxes include council tax, corporation tax, business rates, value added tax, stamp duty land tax and excise duties.

How tax rules are changed

Strangely enough, income tax is a temporary tax and a new Act of Parliament is required each year to allow the government to go on collecting it. This provides the ideal opportunity for the government to ask Parliament to approve changes to the tax rules, so there is an annual cycle.

1 An overview of income tax: what it is, what it means to you and how to pay it

Broadly speaking, income tax is a tax on the regular sums that you receive – for example, earnings from a job, profits from your business, pensions, interest from savings, rental income and so on.

Quick guide

There are many complexities and exceptions in the way that income is taxed. What follows is a broad brush outline. It gives some important relationships:

Adjusted net income = (Income – Reliefs)

Taxable income = (Income – Reliefs – Allowances)

Income tax = Taxable income × The rate(s) of tax

Income is made up of what you earn from your job or self-employment and what you receive as income from other sources, such as pensions and investments. But not all the money you receive is income and some income you receive is tax-free (see next chapter). Some income you receive has had tax deducted called net and some income is paid without tax deducted called gross.

Reliefs are amounts which you pay out and on which you get tax relief, such as pension contributions and donations to charity. Relief may be given in different ways.

Allowances are amounts to which you are entitled because of your personal circumstances.

The income levels at which these rates apply can vary from year to year. Here are the levels of income for each of these rates for 2011–12 and 2012–13:

2011–12 tax year

Income tax band £	Size of band £	Tax rate %
0–2,560	2,560	10[1] or 20
2,561–35,000	32,440	20
35,001–150,000	115,000	40
Over 150,000		50

2012–13 tax year

Income tax band £	Size of band £	Tax rate %
0–2,710	2,710	10[1] or 20
2,711–34,370	31,660	20
34,371–150,000	115,629	40
Over 150,000		50

(1) The 10 per cent rate applies only when this band is set against savings income. If it is set against any other type of income, tax is charged at the basic rate.

1 **Tax-saving idea**   If your income is low, tax that starts at 20 per cent, together with national insurance contributions, takes a large chunk out of any earnings and can make it look as if taking a job would not pay. Make sure you also claim working tax credit which is designed to integrate with the tax system and partially offset the impact of taxes on your take-home pay.

Income

Your income will be made up of money or goods you receive or anything you get in return for a service – but not all payments you receive count as income. The following *will* all normally be considered as income:

- what you earn from your work, including a job, a partnership or self-employment, including salary, tips, fringe benefits and business profits
- rent from letting out property
- income from investments, such as interest, dividends and distributions
- pensions (from the state, your previous employer or your own plan)
- casual, occasional or miscellaneous income, such as freelance earnings, income received after you close a business, income from guaranteeing loans, dealing in futures, income from underwriting, certain capital payments from selling UK patent rights, gains on many discounted securities, accrued income in bond and gilt strip prices
- social security payments, such as Jobseeker's Allowance
- income from a trust.

Payments that are not income

Some payments you receive are not income. For example:

- loans
- presents and gifts (but occasionally inheritance tax may be due later)
- lottery prizes
- gambling winnings
- proceeds from selling assets unless this is how you make a living (but capital gains tax may be due)
- maintenance from an ex-spouse or former partner
- money you inherit (though inheritance tax may have been deducted).

Tax-free income

Some other payments you receive are income but are specifically tax-free, including premium bond prizes, interest on National Savings Certificates and income from savings held in a cash individual savings account (ISA). There is no capital gains tax either on items that are income. A complete list is given in the next chapter.

2 **Tax-saving idea**   Look for opportunities to arrange your income to be tax-free. In the case of a couple, seek to distribute income between the two of you to the greatest advantage.

3 **Tax-saving idea** When you pay into a personal pension or stakeholder scheme, you get tax relief at the basic rate even if you are a non-taxpayer or your top rate of tax is the starting rate.

4 **Tax-saving idea** If you are a higher rate taxpayer and you want a charity to receive £100 in total, you donate £80 which after higher rate relief costs you just £60.

5 **Tax-saving idea** If, say, you have forgotten to claim a relief or allowance, you can go back to correct the past and claim a refund of tax overpaid. You must make your claim within four years of the end of the relevant tax year. So, provided you make your claim by 5 April 2013, you can go back as far as the 2008–09 tax year.

Allowances

Most people are entitled to an allowance to deduct from their income to ensure some of it is tax-free. This is called the personal allowance. The amount of the allowance varies with age and also your adjusted net income.

6 **Tax-saving idea**   Making pension contributions and Gift Aid donations will be especially tax efficient because they also cut your adjusted net income and so increase your age allowance. In effect, you will get tax relief at 30 per cent on such payments.

7 **Tax-saving idea**   If you are 65 (men) or around 60 (women) or older, you might consider deferring your state pension to earn a state pension lump sum. The lump sum does not count as part of your total income and so does not reduce your age allowance.

2 Make the most
of what you earn:
these things are
all free of tax

Income from a job

Check with your employer if you are uncertain about whether any of these forms of income is taxable:

- work-related expenses reimbursed to you by your employer and covered by an agreement with the Revenue that they do not need to be declared
- some fringe benefits, such as canteen meals, mileage allowance up to the authorised rates if you use your own transport for business and certain help with childcare costs
- foreign service allowances paid to diplomats and other servants of the Crown
- goods and services your employer lets you have cheaply
- miners' free coal or cash allowances in lieu of coal
- long-service awards as long as they are not in cash and are within set limits
- awards from approved suggestions schemes
- payments for moving because of your job, within set limits
- genuine personal gifts – for example, wedding presents
- compensation due to medical reasons linked to service in the armed forces, whether or not you continue in service
- armed forces operational allowance paid to members of the armed forces serving in some areas, such as Iraq and Afghanistan

- payments under the Armed Forces Council Tax Relief scheme.

Income on leaving a job

Check with your ex-employer

- gratuities from the armed forces
- payments relating to certain foreign service
- lump-sum compensation for an injury or disability that means you can no longer do the job
- tax-free lump sum instead of part of a pension and certain other *ex gratia* payments on retirement or death
- up to £30,000 of other compensation on leaving a job, including statutory redundancy payments, pay in lieu of notice (provided receiving it was not part of your contract of employment or customary) and counselling and outplacement services.

Pensions and benefits

Check with the organisation paying the pension or benefit

- pension credit, Christmas bonus with state pension, winter fuel payment, cold weather payment
- war widows' and orphans' pensions and equivalent overseas pensions

- bereavement payment
- certain compensation payments and pensions paid to victims of Nazi persecution
- war disablement pensions
- additional pensions paid to holders of some bravery awards, such as the Victoria Cross
- the part of a pension paid to a former employee who retires because of a disability caused by injury at work or a work-related illness that is in excess of the pension paid to an employee who retires on normal ill-health grounds
- income support paid to single parents with a young child and those staying at home to look after a severely disabled person. Part of income support paid to unemployed people may be tax-free – see your statement of taxable benefits
- job finder's grant, most youth training scheme allowances, employment rehabilitation and training allowances, back to work bonus, return to work credit, in work credit, in work emergency discretionary fund payments and in work emergency fund payments
- housing benefit and council tax benefit
- improvement and renovation grants for your home
- payments from the social fund
- maternity allowance (but statutory maternity pay is taxable)
- child benefit, health in pregnancy grant, school uniform grants

- additions for dependent children paid with a state pension or social security benefit
- guardian's allowance
- student grants
- income-related employment and support allowance
- industrial disablement benefits
- disability living allowance
- attendance allowance
- working tax credit and child tax credit, although the amount you get is reduced if your before-tax income exceeds certain thresholds.

Investment income

If in doubt, check with the organisation paying the income

- interest on National Savings & Investment (NS&I) Certificates (and Ulster Savings Certificates, if you normally live in Northern Ireland), NS&I Children's Bonus Bonds
- interest and terminal bonuses on bank and building society Save-As-You-Earn (SAYE) schemes
- income from savings accounts and bond-based investments held in an individual savings account or child trust fund (CTF)
- income from share-based ISAs, CTFs and certain friendly society plans counts as tax-free

- dividends on ordinary shares in a venture capital trust
- part of the income paid by an annuity (other than a pension annuity)
- saving gateway interest and bonus
- loan interest paid to members of a credit union.

Other tax-free income

If in doubt, check with the organisation paying out the money

- what you receive in maintenance payments from a former spouse
- up to £4,250 a year of income from letting out a furnished room in your only or main home – the Rent a Room scheme
- gambling winnings (as long as you are not a bookmaker or similar)
- lottery winnings
- premium bond prizes
- income from qualifying life insurance policies that pay out on death – for example, mortgage protection policies, family income benefit policies
- income from insurance policies to cover mortgage payments if you are sick or unemployed
- income from income protection policies you yourself pay for, creditor insurance and some long-term care policies

- pay-outs under some accident insurance policies (usually group ones)
- interest on a delayed settlement for damages for personal injury or death
- compensation for being wrongly sold a personal pension (but not any interest element of compensation for endowment mis-selling)
- compensation from UK and foreign banks to Holocaust victims and their heirs for assets frozen during World War Two
- interest on a tax rebate
- foster carer's and Shared Lives carer's receipts up to £10,000 a year per household plus £200 a week per child under 11 and £250 a week for children over age 11 and adults
- providing you are not carrying on a trade, income you make from putting into the national grid surplus power from domestic solar panels, wind turbines and other microgeneration methods.

3 How you can pay less tax and how to get it back if you've paid too much

Self assessment started in 1996. It puts the onus on you to report any sources of income and gains, provide a figure for the tax due (though in practice you can ask the Revenue to crunch the numbers for you) and ensure that you make timely payments of the tax due. There are a range of rules and sanctions to discourage cheating. This chapter sets out your legal obligations.

Not everyone has to operate self assessment. Over two-thirds of taxpayers have their tax calculated and collected through PAYE (Pay As You Earn). But even then you need to be aware that a change in their circumstances or a change in the tax system can trigger an obligation under self assessment with the onus on the taxpayer to realise when this occurs.

In addition to policing the system, the Revenue tries to help its customers (taxpayers) to understand the system and operate it correctly. In this role the Revenue tries to put on a friendly public face. Normally a single tax office deals with your affairs, sending you returns, issuing your tax code and so on. But, if you have a query or problem, increasingly you will deal with a website or remote call centre (see Chapter 10 Useful leaflets, forms and contacts).

Your obligations

New source of income or capital

If you don't receive a tax return, you must notify your tax inspector of any income or capital gains, which have not been previously declared, within six months from the end of the tax year in which you make the income or gain (i.e. by 5 October). This applies even if you don't yet know the amount of the income or gain and even if previously you have received a letter from the Revenue saying you do not need to complete a tax return.

There are certain circumstances in which you don't have to notify your tax office. This applies, for example, if all the income comes under the PAYE system or if the income is paid with tax already deducted and you pay tax at no more than the basic rate.

If you fail, within the time limits, to tell the Revenue about your untaxed income or gains, you are liable to a penalty based on the amount of tax owed.

A shorter time limit applies if you become newly self-employed, in which case you must register with the Revenue without delay. There is no precise time limit, but you can be fined if not registering results in tax being paid late and you are deemed to have been careless or dishonest in delaying your registration.

Records

In general you do not have to send in any documents and workings with your tax return. The exception is where you owe capital gains tax (CGT), in which case you do have to include your calculations and the tax return notes provide worksheets for this purpose.

However, you must have and keep records to back up the figures you have reported in your return. To date, this has been a general requirement and it has been up to you to decide which records are relevant, but they will certainly include, for example, end-of-year statements of your employment income (P60s), bank statements, interest certificates, dividend vouchers, and so on. Normally you should keep the originals, but if you don't have them, you can complete your tax return using information that can be verified by an external source. You should also keep any working papers that you have used to make your calculations. Under a recent change in the law, the Revenue has new powers to specify exactly which records you must keep. The records which need to be kept, and the circumstances in which you need to keep them, are listed by the Revenue at www.hmrc.gov.uk/sa/record-keeping.htm.

You must normally keep these records for one year from the 31 January following the end of the tax year covered by the return. But, if you run your own business or have letting income, the period is five years. The Revenue can override these rules and specify an earlier date.

This period is extended if there is an enquiry into your affairs. Records must be kept until the enquiry is complete. The period to keep records is also extended if you send in your return late or need to correct it after you have sent it in. The documents need to be kept until one year after the end of the quarter in which you amended the return or sent it in late. Quarters end on 31 January, 30 April, 31 July and 31 October.

The failure to keep records can result in a heavy penalty.

8 **Tax-saving idea** Make sure you keep all your records and your working papers. If you don't, you may end up paying more tax than you should because you can't provide the evidence to back up your tax return. And don't forget you can be fined for not keeping your records. If you are in business or letting, you must normally keep your records for two years. Other taxpayers must keep records for that year for six years.

The tax return

Your current tax return asks for details of your income, deductions and allowances for the tax year just ended, that is the year ending at the beginning of April. Roughly 1.5 million people with straightforward tax affairs are sent a short four-page tax return. If your affairs are more complex, you will receive the full return comprising a six-page main return accompanied by additional forms and supplements. It is your responsibility to check that you have received the correct tax return and supplements and to obtain the right form and any other supplements you need.

You must provide precise figures throughout your return. This means getting hold of the documents you need. If you are an employee, these include forms P60 (summary of income from a job and tax already paid), P45 (summary of income and tax paid where you have left a job), P11D or P9D (taxable fringe benefits and expenses). Your employer is responsible for supplying you with these forms by certain dates. Where precise figures are not available (for example, where you are self-employed and the relevant accounting period has yet to end), give a provisional estimate and say when the final figure will be available. With subjective figures (for example, the value of an asset you have given away or received from your employer), get an independent valuation and give details in the *Any other information* sections of the return.

If figures on returns from taxpayers like you are commonly subject to errors, or based on previous years your figures seem out of step with those for similar taxpayers, you may receive a letter from the Revenue suggesting you take particular care in completing that section of your return.

In general, you do not need to send supporting documents with your tax return. If you wish to draw the Revenue's attention to an item or explain the basis of your figures, it is normally best to make a note in the *Any other information* boxes provided on the main return and its supplements. If you do send supporting documents, it is unlikely that they will be read unless your tax office decides to open an enquiry into your return.

Deadlines for your tax return

For your tax return, there are two key dates. Which one is important for you depends on how you file your return:

• **The end of October**. This is the date by which you must send in a paper tax return. The Revenue will work out your tax bill for you. If you file a paper return after this date, you normally incur an automatic fine.

- **The end of January**. This is the final deadline for the
  return and there is an automatic fine if you miss it. To
  take advantage of this later date, you must file your
  tax return online and the software will automatically
  calculate your tax bill.

If the amount of tax you owe is less than £2,000, you can
agree to have it collected through PAYE during the course
of the following year, provided you file a paper return by 31
October or an online return by 30 December.

9 **Tax-saving idea**   If you are paying tax under the PAYE
system and have some other income, for example from
investments, on which you will need to pay tax, send in
your tax return by 31 October or 30 December if you file
by internet. If you do this, and the amount of tax due is
less than £2,000, it will be included in your PAYE code for
the following tax year, thus spreading out and delaying
the payment.

10 **Tax-saving idea**   If you prefer to complete a paper tax
return, make sure you send it in by 31 October following
the end of the tax year to avoid paying a fine.

Filing by internet

Filing by internet is free if you use the Revenue's own software.

The main advantages of online filing are that the software prompts you to correct common errors, immediately tells you the amount of tax you owe, immediately states whether your return has been received and gives you the option to pay tax in instalments by direct debit.

To file online you must first register, which can take up to seven working days. Follow the instructions supplied with your return or on the Revenue website. You can also pay tax electronically – see the Revenue website for details.

In 2009, the Revenue warned of a big increase in fraudulent claims for tax repayments, often using passwords and other information obtained from taxpayers. Beware of so-called 'phishing' emails that purport to be from the Revenue and ask for sensitive information or instruct you to click on a link. The Revenue will never ask you for passwords or request bank details in this way. If you receive such emails, do not open them or click on any links. Forward such emails to phishing@hmrc.gsi.gov.uk and then delete them.

11 **Tax-saving idea**   Online filing gives you an extra three months to sort out your tax return and is free if you use the Revenue's own software. Commercial software prices start at around £18 for the full tax return.

12 **Tax-saving idea**   If you are new to the Revenue's online filing software, do not leave sorting out your tax return to the last minute. It will be too late to send in a paper return and you must register before you can use the online service. This takes around seven working days. There is normally an automatic penalty if you file your return late. If you run a business in partnership with others, note that you can use the free Revenue software to file your own partnership supplement online but not the partnership return itself.

If you don't send in your tax return

Failing to send back your completed tax return means you can be charged a penalty and allows the Revenue to issue what's called a determination. This is an estimate of the tax you might owe and is often deliberately on the high side. The tax shown on this determination is payable; you cannot appeal against it or postpone it. The only way you can overturn this estimate is to complete your tax return and tax calculation. From 1 April 2010 onwards, you must do this within three years of the date by which you should have filed the return (before 1 April 2010, the time limit was five years) or, if it is later, within a year of the determination by your tax inspector.

If you miss this deadline, you must normally pay the amount of tax stated in the determination. However, if you can show this is excessive compared with what you would have had to pay had you sent in a return on time, you may be able to get the tax bill reduced to the amount that would have been payable. If you think this may apply in your case, contact your tax office or a tax adviser.

The Revenue must normally issue a determination within three years (was five years) of the normal filing date for the missing return. But if there is reason to think that the failure to file is due to carelessness, the limit is extended to six years or, if due to a deliberate attempt to avoid paying tax, 20 years.

Tax calculation

After you have sent in a paper tax return, the Revenue checks it for obvious errors, such as arithmetical mistakes or failing to copy figures correctly from one part to another. You will be sent a tax calculation form (SA302), unless you have opted to calculate your own tax bill (and we recommend you don't). The form sets out the tax the Revenue thinks you owe and the amount of any payments you have to make. Check this carefully as soon as it arrives. If there is anything you do not understand, or you disagree with the figures, write to or phone your tax office – otherwise you will be expected to pay the amounts shown on the form. If you file online, the software will immediately tell you the amount of tax you owe and when it is due to be paid.

13 **Tax-saving idea**   Always check tax forms, such as a tax calculation or coding notice, to make sure your tax office has got the sums right. Under rules that apply to tax returns from 2008–09 onwards, you may be charged a penalty if the Revenue makes an error that results in you paying too little tax and you fail to alert your tax office to the error within 30 days.

Tax payments

Self assessment is used to collect income tax, capital gains tax and, if you are in business, class 4 national insurance contributions (NICs). You, your adviser or your tax inspector work out the total amount due. The tax is usually paid in three instalments.

Interim and final payments

Self assessment requires two interim payments on account. The first is due on 31 January during the tax year; the second on 31 July following the tax year. Each payment is normally half the amount of your income tax and class 4 NICs bill for the previous year less any tax paid through the PAYE system, dividend tax credits and so on. There is no adjustment for changes in tax rates and allowances from one year to the next. However, if you expect your income to be lower this year than last, you can ask for a reduction in the payments on account – but, if you turn out to be wrong, you'll have to pay interest on the tax paid late.

The final balancing income tax payment or repayment will be made on 31 January following the end of the tax year after completion of the tax return. Any capital gains tax due will also be paid with this third instalment.

Employees can put off paying a final tax bill of less than £2,000 by agreeing to have it included in next year's PAYE code. If filing a paper return, this happens automatically unless you opt out.

An effect of the self assessment payment system is that, if your income increases from one tax year to the next, you may face a hefty tax bill in the following January. This is because the jump in income produces a final payment to scoop up tax underpaid in the last tax year plus an increased payment on account for the current tax year.

Conversely, if your income falls from one year to the next, there may be a large drop in your January tax payment if you stand to get a refund of tax overpaid and a lower first payment on account.

14 **Tax-saving idea**   If your income is increasing year on year, expect a large tax bill in January comprising your final payment and an increased payment on account. Make sure you set aside enough money to pay this bill, otherwise you risk interest charges on tax paid late and possibly penalties too.

Self assessment statement

Shortly before a payment on account falls due, you will usu-ally receive a self assessment statement (form SA300) showing the amount to pay and with a pay slip attached. If you are registered for the Revenue's internet service, you can view recent statements online.

These statements are personalised. The key figure is the 'Amount due by …', which shows what you must pay and when. Paying late means paying interest, so it's vital to check your statements.

How to reduce your payments

If you think your tax bill this year will be lower than in the previous year, you can claim to make lower payments on account than the Revenue is asking for. This can happen because your income has dropped – for example you are getting less in profits or rents. Or maybe you have become newly eligible for a tax allowance or extra relief, for example because you have reached age 65 or increased your pension contributions.

If this is the case, carefully work out your expected tax bill for this year (including class 4 national insurance if you are self-employed). Halve the total to find the amount for each payment on account. Then fill in form SA303, which you can get from your tax office or the Revenue website at www.hmrc.gov.uk or make your claim for a reduction online. To reduce a forthcoming payment, return the form before the 'due by' date on the self assessment statement. If later you realise you will owe even less tax, you can make another claim, again using form SA303.

15 **Tax-saving idea**   Always check your self assessment statement to see if you can claim a reduction in the interim payments on account. But, if in doubt, it is better to pay slightly more than to ask for a reduction. You will be charged interest if you pay too little, whereas tax you have overpaid may earn interest. The interest charged on underpaid tax is much higher than that added to overpaid tax. You can also be fined if you knowingly reduce your payments on account by too much.

Interest and surcharges

Provided you pay the original payments on account demanded on time, no interest is normally charged even if your tax bill for the year turns out to be much higher. In other cases, interest is payable on tax paid late. On the other hand, any tax you have overpaid usually earns interest. Any interest charged or received will be shown on your self assessment statement.

From mid-2009 onwards, interest is set by the Revenue in line with the Bank of England base rate:

• on tax paid late, interest is set at the Bank of England base rate plus 2.5 per cent

- on tax overpaid, the rate is the Bank of England base rate minus 1 per cent but subject to a minimum rate of 0.5 per cent.

Interest is automatically charged on any tax left unpaid after the 31 January or 31 July payment deadlines.

How to pay

The Revenue has been expanding the methods available for paying tax. To pay a tax bill that is already due, you can choose between:

- sending a cheque by post
- paying cash, cheque or debit card at any Post Office or your own bank or building society branch
- using phone or internet banking to transfer the payment direct from your own to the Revenue's bank account. The payslip or payment reminder you receive includes the Revenue bank account details that you will need
- paying by internet using a debit or credit card. For how to do this, see www.billpayment.co.uk/hmrc/scripts/index.asp. If you use a credit card, you must also pay a transaction fee
- paying over the internet by direct debit, provided you are registered for the Revenue's internet filing service
- buying certificates of tax deposit (see www.hmrc.gov.uk/payinghmrc/cert-tax-deposit.htm). These work rather like buying savings stamps. The minimum you can have saved with certificates of tax deposit at any time

is £500 and you can buy further certificates in amounts of at least £250.

If you use the Revenue's online filing service, you also have the option of setting up a budget payment plan which is a direct debit to make regular weekly or monthly payments that reduce your next tax bill. To be eligible your current tax payments must be up to date. You cannot withdraw the advance payments you have already made but you can, at any time, alter the amount of your future payments, suspend them for up to six months or cancel the plan. Your advance payments do not earn interest.

16 **Tax-saving idea** A budget payment plan or buying certificates of tax deposit can help you plan for future tax bills and so avoid late payment penalties. Financially you may be better off setting up a direct debit to pay regular savings into a bank or building society account that pays interest on your savings, but you need to be confident you would not withdraw the money to use for anything other than your tax bill.

17 **Tax-saving idea** Failing to pay tax on time results in interest charges and penalties and the Revenue is quick to chase late payments. If you are having problems paying your tax bill, contact your tax office straight away. You may be able to negotiate an agreement, for example to pay by instalments and avoid penalty charges.

18 **Tax-saving idea**   To help businesses the Revenue has launched a new Business Payment Support Service. If you anticipate that you will not be able to pay your tax on time, the Revenue may agree a tailored package to pay the tax owed on dates or in stages that match your cash flow. Interest will be added to tax paid late, but no penalties or surcharges will be incurred. To find out more, see www. hmrc.gov.uk/payinghmrc/problems/bpps.htm or call the Business Payment Support Line on 0845 302 1435.

The PAYE system

Your employer or private pension provider is an unpaid tax collector for the Revenue using the PAYE system – Pay As You Earn. Every time employees or pensioners are paid, income tax and national insurance contributions are deducted from the earnings or pension and sent in a batch to the collector of taxes. Your employer is also responsible for collecting student loan repayments on behalf of the government through your pay packet.

Your employer or pension provider needs various bits of information to operate the PAYE system, in particular a PAYE code for each employee or pensioner. This is issued by the Revenue and tells the employer or pension provider how much tax-free pay to give you each month or week. The Revenue also sends you a notice of your PAYE code, for example in January or February in time for the coming tax

year or when your circumstances change. You will not nec-
essarily get a notice every year. You can request a coding
notice at any time.

19 **Tax-saving idea** According to the National Audit Office
(a body that keeps a watch on the government's money
management), around three out of ten tax coding notices
contain errors. If your PAYE code is wrong, you may pay
too much tax and have to wait for a rebate. And, although
paying too little tax might seem attractive, you will have
to make up any underpayment in the following tax year –
often in one go if it is £2,000 or more. So it makes sense
to check your PAYE code carefully whenever you receive
a notice of coding.

The coding notice

The coding notice (form P2) sets out the Revenue's calculations to arrive at your PAYE code. Your employer uses the
code in conjunction with tax tables supplied by the Revenue
to work out how much tax to deduct from your pay.

If you work for two employers, you should have two PAYE
codes – one for each job – and two coding notices. If you are
retired and receive an occupational and/or personal pension, you will also have tax deducted through PAYE. If you
have just one main pension, you'll get one PAYE code. If you
have two or more substantial pensions, you may get a code
for each one.

Your employer usually makes various other adjustments to your gross salary to arrive at your take-home pay. These can include deduction of national insurance, student loan repayments, pension contributions and donations to charity through payroll giving. None of these is reflected in your PAYE code.

Claiming a tax refund

If you have paid too much tax through PAYE because you have stopped doing a job part way through the tax year, a refund will be arranged automatically by your new employer or the Jobcentre Plus office handling your benefit claim. But, if you are neither going to a new job nor getting benefit, claim a tax rebate using form P50.

In other cases where you have paid too much tax – for example, because tax has been deducted from your savings income but you are a non-taxpayer – claim a refund using form R40. Do not send any documents, such as certificates of tax deducted, with the form but keep them safe in case your tax office asks to see them. The Revenue normally aims to process your claim within 28 days. You do not have to wait until the end of the tax year to make a claim but repayments of less than £50 are not usually made mid-year.

Either ask your tax office for the relevant claim form or download it from www.hmrc.gov.uk. You can't submit these forms online.

Take care when claiming tax back. If you make an error, you are liable for the same penalties as apply to mistakes made in a tax return.

PAYE and students

Increasingly, students take on some paid work to help finance their way through college. If you expect to earn less than your personal allowance and will be working only during the holidays, you may be able to arrange to be paid gross by completing form P38(S), available from the Revenue website. However, the employer does not have to agree to this and can opt instead to pay you through PAYE in the normal way.

You cannot use the P38(S) system if you work during term time.

Being taxed through PAYE means you can pay too much tax. There are ways to get it back:

- if you take another job during the tax year, you may get a refund through PAYE operated by your new employer. This is most likely if you can give the new employer a P45 (a form you should be given when you leave a job, summarising your tax and pay from that job)

- you can claim a refund once the tax year has ended by contacting your tax office (which will be shown on your tax or pay documents)

- you may be able to claim one or more refunds during the course of the tax year using form P50 available from the Revenue website.

20 **Tax-saving idea**   Students can check whether they may be due a tax refund by using the Revenue calculator at www.hmrc.gov.uk/calcs/stc.htm.

21 **Tax-saving idea**   Make a point of asking for a P45 when you leave a job. If you take another job, giving your new employer the P45 will help to ensure that you get a refund of any overpaid tax and do not overpay in the new job.

4 What if you have tax problems? Solutions for dealing with them

Given the complexity of the UK tax system, it is hardly surprising if your tax affairs do not always run smoothly. Here are some ideas on how to cope with the most common problems you are likely to face.

Changes to your tax return

Estimates, mistakes and corrections

There are several reasons for wanting to alter a tax return after you have sent it in. If a change results in extra tax being due, you will be charged interest on the tax paid late and you may have to pay a penalty if you have made an error which is deemed careless or deliberate.

If you have put a provisional figure in your return, you must supply the final figure as soon as it is known.

You might make a mistake when you complete the return. You have 12 months from the filing date within which you can amend your return with a minimum of fuss. Simply phone or write to your usual tax office explaining the amendment required. If, within nine months of the date you sent in the return, the Revenue picks up any obvious errors, it too can amend the return.

You also have an additional time period to correct any mistakes and claim back any tax overpaid as a result. From 1 April 2010, this period is four years following the end of the tax year.

Interventions

Since July 2006, the Revenue has been using a range of informal methods to help taxpayers get their tax right where the Revenue suspects there may be problems. These 'interventions' can take the form of letters, phone calls or visits. The Revenue may ask you to review the way you keep your business records, fill in a questionnaire to review the tax-compliance risks you face, or reconsider particular entries on your tax return. Where it has third party information, the Revenue may correct your tax return and ask you to explain the perceived error and to take steps to avoid it happening again. So far, it is up to you to choose whether to take part in these interventions.

Enquiries

Your tax office has the right to open a formal enquiry into your tax return. A small proportion of all returns is selected at random for enquiry. But most are chosen because the Revenue thinks there is something wrong or a risk assessment analysis suggests there is a high chance of this. Your tax office must tell you if the enquiry is into your whole return or just some aspect of it (such as a particular expense you have claimed).

Your tax office must give you written notice of an enquiry. The enquiry must normally start within one year of the date on which you filed your return. If your return was late or you amended it, the enquiry deadline is extended to one year from the end of the calendar quarter in which you sent in your late or amended return.

Your tax office has the right to demand that you produce certain documents as part of the enquiry. When you receive a notice of an enquiry, you may also receive a notice to produce these within 30 days. You can provide copies, but your tax inspector may insist on seeing the originals. You can appeal within 30 days against this notice to produce documents.

You can also appeal to the First-Tier Tribunal if you consider that an enquiry should not have been undertaken or is being continued unnecessarily. If it agrees, the tribunal can issue a notice to the Revenue requiring it to close the enquiry.

When the subject of an enquiry is complete, your tax office will issue you with a formal notice telling you so, how much tax you are considered to owe, any penalty charge, and requiring you to amend your self assessment. You can appeal against it, if you don't agree. The result of a tax enquiry may also lead to a revision of any tax credits you claim. Once the enquiry is closed, no further enquiry can be made into the same return but a discovery assessment is possible. For more information about enquiry procedures and your rights, see Revenue booklet IR160 *Enquiries under Self Assessment* or www.hmrc.gov.uk/pdfs/ir160.pdf.

Discovery assessments

The aim of the enquiry process was to give you, the taxpayer, certainty about when the assessment for a tax year had become final and could be consigned to the archives. However, the Revenue can reopen a past return even after the enquiry window has passed, if it discovers that more tax should have been paid and either you are deemed to have acted carelessly or deliberately or your tax office could not reasonably have known on the basis of the information available at the time that extra tax was due. In these situations, the Revenue can send you a discovery assessment setting out the amount of extra tax it thinks you now owe.

Currently, the Revenue must normally make any discovery assessment within four years after the end of the tax year. However, the limit is extended to six years if you are deemed to have been careless, and 20 years if you deliberately withheld information.

22 **Tax-saving idea**   If the outcome of an enquiry or appeal against a discovery assessment is that you have to pay extra tax, interest will be added to reflect the fact the tax is being paid late. However, at the start of the enquiry or appeal, if you buy a certificate of tax deposit to cover the amount of tax in dispute, interest stops accruing from the date you buy the certificate. If the dispute is settled in your favour, you can exchange the certificate for cash.

Information checks

Since 1 April 2009, you can be asked to provide a tax officer with any information and documents reasonably required for the purpose of checking your tax position. This is an extremely wide power that can mean virtually any type of information or document and can relate to your past, present or future tax liabilities. The information need not be linked to a tax return, so can focus on how adequately you are maintaining your records on a day-to-day basis. It can also apply not just to UK tax, but also taxes levied by other European Union states or other countries with which the UK has tax agreements.

The Revenue must send you a written notice requesting this information and/or documents (called an 'information notice'), giving a reasonable time limit for their production. You can provide copies, unless the notice specifies that you must supply originals. You and the Revenue may agree a place where the information and documents can be inspected. Alternatively, the Revenue can select a venue but this cannot be somewhere used solely as a private home. The Revenue may copy or retain documents (giving you a receipt for them).

The Revenue also has wide powers to request information from third parties to help in checking your tax position. The tax officer should normally ask for your agreement before contacting a third party.

23 **Tax-saving idea** The Revenue's powers to specify which records must be kept and to require information and to inspect documents at any time put pressure on you to keep your records up to date, especially if you are running a small business. Stuffing documents in an old carrier bag to be sorted out after the end of the tax year is likely to be interpreted by the Revenue as, at best, careless. It could trigger enquiries and discovery assessments with possible back-tax, interest and penalties to pay. Try to get into the habit of organising your book-keeping and relevant tax records on at least a weekly basis.

Penalties, appeals and complaints

Penalties

The self assessment system is underpinned by a range of penalties. In addition, interest is added to overdue tax and also to penalties that remain unpaid. Your tax office has discretion to reduce some penalties based on, for example, the gravity of your case and the extent of your co-operation.

The penalty system is being reviewed and updated in stages. For returns submitted from April 2009 onwards (in other words covering tax periods from 2008–09 onwards), a new range of penalties applies if your tax return or any related documents, such as business accounts, are incorrect. Penalties are chargeable if the error is either deliberate or due to carelessness. You are expected to take reasonable care both when you prepare your return and when you check documents sent to you by someone acting for you. This means you can be penalised for an error made by a tax adviser or even by the Revenue itself.

The penalties are set by reference to the amount of tax you owe and there are three levels. The maximum penalty may be reduced if you co-operate in disclosing and correcting the error. The Revenue can also suspend a penalty for up to two years if you agree to make changes aimed at avoiding a repeat of the error.

Incorrect return or failure to notify: size of penalty as a percentage of tax owed

	Type of error		
	Careless or Revenue error	Deliberate not concealed	Deliberate with steps taken to conceal it
Maximum penalty	30%	70%	100%
Minimum penalty if unprompted you disclose the error[1]	0%[2]	20%	30%
Minimum penalty if prompted you disclose the error[1]	15%[2]	35%	50%

(1) The size of the reduction depends on the extent to which you co-operate with the Revenue, for example by providing information.
(2) Amounts shown in the table apply to incorrect return. In the case of failure to notify a new source of income or gain, the minimum penalties are: unprompted disclosure, 10 per cent (or 0 per cent if disclosure is within 12 months of tax becoming due); prompted disclosure, 20 per cent (or 10 per cent if disclosure is within 12 months of tax becoming due).

24 **Tax-saving idea**   Don't be late sending in your tax return. The paper return must be sent back by 31 October and online returns by 31 January to avoid an automatic £100 penalty.

In 2001, a criminal offence was introduced of being '*knowingly concerned in the fraudulent evasion of income tax*'. This is aimed at catching people who deliberately dodge tax, for example employers and employees colluding to pay less through PAYE, or householders and tradespeople deliberately negotiating a cash price so they benefit from tax saved. The maximum penalty for serious cases is an unlimited fine and/or seven years in prison.

Appeals and complaints

You can appeal against the following: an assessment that is not a self assessment, an amendment to your self assessment by the Revenue after an enquiry, an amendment of a partnership statement where a loss of tax is discovered, a disallowance in whole or in part of a claim or election included in a tax return, penalty determinations, or a formal notice requesting documents or entry to business premises.

25 **Tax-saving idea**   You can appeal against the £100 penalty for missing the deadline for sending in your tax return, by writing to your tax office. You would need a reasonable excuse, for example an unexpected postal strike, serious illness, the death of a close relative, or loss of records due to fire, flood or theft. Pressure of work, a failure by your tax adviser or lack of information would not be regarded as a reasonable excuse. If you have tried to file online but the software has rejected your return, this may qualify as a reasonable excuse provided you send your tax office the error message or error code produced by the software.

You have to give written notice of appeal within 30 days after the issue of the notice of assessment, amendment or disallowance.

If you disagree about the amount of the tax bill, you should first of all exhaust the avenues within the Revenue by asking for an internal review – your tax office may take the first step and offer you this option. In general, the Revenue must then set out its initial view of the matter within 30 days and then have to complete the review within a further 45 days. Where possible, the review should be carried out by different tax officials from those involved in the original decision. If you do not agree with the outcome of the internal review, you have 30 days within which to appeal to the tribunal. You do not have to go through the Revenue internal review process, but can go straight to the tribunal if you prefer.

5 Tax and your home

In general, the tax system treats you as an independent person. But there are special rules designed to help (or sometimes to prevent tax avoidance) where particular circumstances relate to you or your household. This applies, for example, if you are married, in a civil partnership, have children or are on a low income.

Marriage and civil partnerships

Married couples and civil partners are treated as two independent entities for the purpose of paying tax. Each person is taxed on their own income and gains and has their own allowances. Each is responsible for filling in their own tax return and paying their own tax bills. There is no longer a tax allowance for married couples unless either or both husband and wife were born before 6 April 1935 – this allowance is also available to older civil partners.

However, there are some aspects of the tax system which recognise that husband and wife, or civil partners, are more than just two individuals living together. One is that they can transfer some allowances between them in certain circumstances. Gifts between them don't normally trigger a capital gains tax or inheritance tax bill. And by sharing their wealth, a couple can each use their tax-free allowances to reduce the amounts paid in tax.

26 **Tax-saving idea**   If one of you pays tax at a higher rate than the other, or one of you is losing personal allowance and the other has income under £100,000, consider giving investments which produce a taxable income to the spouse or civil partner who would pay least tax on the income.

27 **Tax-saving idea**   Gifts between married couples or civil partners must be genuine with no strings attached. If you are reluctant to give away the investments completely, consider putting them into joint names so the income is shared equally.

28 **Tax-saving idea**   Since 5 December 2005, same-sex couples who register their relationship as a civil partnership are treated for tax in the same way as married couples.

Jointly owned assets

If you have investments which are jointly owned, your tax officer will assume the income from them is split equally between you. If the investments are not owned in equal proportions, you can have the income divided between you to reflect your actual shares of it.

Personal allowances

A husband, wife and civil partner are each entitled to a personal tax allowance in the same way as single people – usually £6,475 in 2010–11, £7,475 in 2011–12 and £8,105 in 2012–13.

Married couple's allowance

Married couple's allowance is given only where one (or both) of a couple was born before 6 April 1935.

The allowance gives tax relief at 10 per cent as a reduction in the tax bill.

29 **Tax-saving idea**   Is one of you 75 or over? And does whichever of you gets the age-related part of the married couple's allowance have adjusted net income high enough to be losing part of the allowance? You may be able to save tax by transferring investments that produce income to the other spouse or partner.

Transfer of allowances because of low income

If either spouse or civil partner has a tax bill that is too low to use up all their married couple's allowance, they can ask to have the unused part deducted from the tax bill of their spouse or partner. Even the age-related addition can be transferred in these circumstances. You can do this after the end of the tax year in which you got the allowance. You can go back four years if, in the past, you had not realised you could transfer the allowance in this way.

30 **Tax-saving idea** If your income is too low to use all the married couple's allowance, even the age-related part can be transferred to your spouse or civil partner.

31 **Tax-saving idea** Married couples and civil partners of any age can transfer blind person's allowance between them if the recipient has too little income to be able to use the allowance fully. The unused part can be transferred to the spouse or partner even if they themselves are not blind.

Separation and divorce/ dissolving a partnership

Separation, divorce or dissolving a civil partnership may affect:

- tax relief on maintenance you pay, but only if you or your spouse or partner were born before 6 April 1935

- national insurance contributions you pay if you are a married woman who has been paying contributions at the married women's reduced rate

- your entitlement to tax credits
- the tax allowances you get in the year it happens, but only if you or your spouse or partner were born before 6 April 1935.

If any of the above apply to you, you should tell your tax officer when you separate (and within one month for tax credits), even if you have not yet made a formal deed of separation or sought a court order. The Revenue will then treat you as no longer living with your spouse or partner, provided your circumstances suggest that the separation will be permanent.

Maintenance payments

Maintenance can take several forms, including direct payments of cash or the provision of support such as a home to live in. The person receiving maintenance does not pay any tax on the amount they get.

National insurance contributions

Paying certain types of national insurance contributions entitles you to some state benefits, such as state retirement pension. If you are a woman and you married before May 1977, you may have opted to pay contributions at the 'married women's reduced rate'. In return for paying less national insurance, you gave up the right to those state benefits and instead relied on your husband.

Your right to pay national insurance at the reduced rate ends at the time your marriage ends – generally, on the date of the decree absolute. If you are an employee, tell your employer so that he can arrange for you to pay full rate contributions. If you are self-employed, notify your tax office.

Capital gains tax and inheritance tax on separation

You can carry on making gifts to your ex-spouse or ex-partner in the year of separation without falling into the net for capital gains tax. After this, gifts may lead to a capital gains tax bill in the same way as for any other gifts.

However, if you move out of the family home and later dispose of the property or your share in it as part of the divorce settlement, there is no capital gains tax to pay, provided: your former spouse or partner continues to live there as their only or main home; and you have not elected for any other property to be your only or main home. For example, you might consider renting until the sale or transfer of the home is sorted out.

Gifts between separated spouses or separated civil partners are normally free of inheritance tax. Once you are divorced or the partnership is dissolved, gifts may fall into the inheritance tax net unless they are for the maintenance of the ex-spouse, ex-partner or any children.

Bereavement

If your husband, wife or civil partner dies, you carry on getting your own personal allowance as usual. If you have been claiming tax credits, within one month of becoming bereaved you need to make a new claim as a single person.

Living together

If you live with someone without being married or registered as a civil partnership, you are treated for tax purposes as single people. However, the same is not true for tax credits. The amount of any tax credits you can claim depends on your household income and couples are treated as being part of the same household whether or not they are married.

Children and young people

In general, the tax system does not treat people differently on the grounds of age. Therefore a child, just like an adult, has their own income tax allowance, tax bands and capital gains tax allowance. However, there are some rules specific to children and young people, in particular:

- to counter tax avoidance, where a parent gives money or investments to a child and these produce an income, that income is taxed as the income of the parent not the child unless it comes to no more than £100 a year. The £100 limit applies per parent per child

- individual savings accounts are generally not available to people under age 18 except that young people may hold cash ISAs from age 16 onwards

- some payments commonly received by young people and students are tax-free – these include: educational maintenance allowance; student loans, grants and bursaries; and most youth training scheme allowances

- although children can be taxpayers, until they reach age 16 they have no liability for national insurance on any earnings or profits.

32 **Tax-saving idea**   If you give capital to your children and it produces over £100 income a year, that income will normally be taxed as yours. Choose investments that produce a tax-free income instead (see Chapter 6).

33 **Tax-saving idea**   If you are a student, claim back any tax deducted from earnings and claim back any tax deducted from savings using form R40. Arrange to have savings interest paid without tax deducted by giving the bank or building society form R85. If you work only in the holidays, arrange to get your wages paid gross by filling in form P38S. All forms are available from tax offices and the Revenue website, www.hmrc.gov.uk.

34 **Tax-saving idea**   As a school or college student, you are likely to be a non-taxpayer, so you may think there is no point using the ISA allowance you get from age 16 onwards. But, once you have invested in an ISA, those savings are sheltered indefinitely from tax. So the protection from tax will continue even after you start work and become a taxpayer.

Households with children or on a low income

If you are working and have a low income or if you have children (in which case you do not need to be working and can have a fairly substantial income), you may be eligible for tax credits.

35 **Tax-saving idea**   Households with children and an income up to £41,360 are eligible for child tax credit. This is not given automatically.

36 **Tax-saving idea**   Even with an income just over £40,000, you can qualify for working tax credit if you pay for childcare. However, you may instead be able to get help with childcare costs from your employer.

37 **Tax-saving idea**   Your tax credit claim is initially based on your income for the previous year and is adjusted only if your income for the current year is higher by more than £10,000. This means, if your income was low last year – for example, due to a period of unemployment – you may still be eligible for tax credits this tax year even if you are now back in work.

Tax and your home

Running a business or letting your home

If you use your home for business purposes, you may be able to set off some of the interest against business income.

If you take out or extend a mortgage against your home and use the money raised in your business or to finance property you rent out, you can claim part of the interest as an allowable expense.

If you let part or all of your home, you may be able to deduct mortgage interest when working out your profit or loss.

Capital gains tax on homes

If you sell most types of investments (including property) for more than you paid for them, there may be capital gains tax to pay. But if you sell your only or main home, there is normally no capital gains tax. This exemption is known as private residence relief.

Which homes?

Private residence relief is given for your only or main home, whether it is a house or flat, freehold or leasehold, and wherever in the world it is.

You must occupy the home exclusively as your residence if it is to be free of capital gains tax. If part of the home is used exclusively for business, you may have to pay tax on part of the gain. And letting out some or all of your home can also mean a capital gains tax bill.

If you live in a caravan or houseboat, there's normally no capital gains tax to pay on it, even if it is not your only or main home. Caravans and boats count as wasting assets with a useful life of 50 years or less – and are thus outside the net for capital gains tax. But if you own the land on which a caravan stands, you might have to pay capital gains tax if you sell it, unless the caravan was your only or main home.

Gains on a former home that continues to be occupied by your ex-spouse are tax-free if you sell within three years of your leaving. A longer exemption period applies if this is your ex-spouse's only or main home and you have not nominated any other property as your own only or main home.

A home in which a dependent relative lives rent-free is also free of capital gains tax provided it fell into this category on or before 5 April 1988. This exemption lasts only as long as the relative continues to live in the home. Dependent relatives are: your mother or the mother of your spouse or civil partner if she is widowed, separated or divorced; any relative of yours or your spouse or civil partner who is unable to look after themselves because of permanent illness, disablement or old age (usually 65 or over).

If you have more than one home

If you have more than one home, you can choose which is your main one and so free of capital gains tax. It doesn't have to be the home where you spend most time.

38 **Tax-saving idea** If you have more than one home, you can nominate which one is to be treated as your main home for tax purposes. Normally, choose the one on which you expect to make the largest gain.

39 **Tax-saving idea** Married couples and registered civil partners must nominate just one home between them as their main home. But unmarried and unregistered partners can each elect a different residence as their main home even if, say, one is used only for weekends.

40 **Tax-saving idea** Every time the number of homes you have – whether or not you own them – changes you have a new opportunity to elect your main home. You could create a new opportunity by, for example, renting a flat for a few weeks. This could be worth doing if you previously missed the two-year time limit for electing which of two homes should count as your main home.

Working from home

If any part of your home is used exclusively for business, there may be a capital gains tax bill when you sell the home. This will not usually apply if you are an employee working from home, but could do if a substantial part of your home is set aside exclusively for the work.

If you use one or more rooms entirely for business (as an office or workshop, for example), there will be tax on part of the gain when you sell the home. You will have to agree the proportion with the tax officer, who may base it on the number of rooms you use or market value if the business part could be sold separately. If you claim part of the mortgage interest as a business expense, the same proportion of the gain is likely to be taxable.

41 **Tax-saving idea**   If you work from home, you can avoid capital gains tax on the home when you come to sell if you ensure that you do not use part of your home exclusively for business – for example, you use a home-office also for domestic purposes. But, in that case, you will have to scale back the home-related business expenses you claim each year in line with the non-business use.

42 **Tax-saving idea**   If you are away from home for quite long periods, keep an eye on the capital gains tax position so that you don't lose private residence relief.

Capital gains tax on lettings

There is no capital gains tax to pay if you take in one lodger who is treated as a member of the family – sharing your living rooms and eating with you. But in other circumstances, there may be capital gains tax to pay when you sell a home that has been let out wholly or in part.

If you let out the whole house for a period, the gain attributable to that period is taxable.

43 **Tax-saving idea**   You can claim letting relief only in respect of a residence that has been your main home at some time. So, if you buy a property mainly to let out, it could be worth moving in and making it your home for a while. There is no minimum time period but you must be able to prove that it was genuinely your permanent home while you were there.

Inheritance

If you inherit a property – for example, a family home on the death of your parents – you are deemed to have acquired it at its market value on the date of death. If you do not take up residence, there could be capital gains tax to pay if you sell the property and its value has risen since the date of death.

6 Savings, investments and pensions: How to make the most of putting money away

To encourage savings, the government offers various tax incentives to investors, including tax relief on pension contributions and special tax rules to persuade you to build up savings for yourself (individual savings accounts – ISAs) or your children (junior ISAs) and invest in new businesses (for example venture capital trusts).

Income tax on investments

Interest paid after deduction of tax

Interest on most kinds of savings is now normally paid after tax has been deducted from it. This applies to building society accounts, bank accounts, annuities (other than pension annuities), local authority loans and bonds and National Savings & Investments (NS&I) guaranteed income and guaranteed growth bonds.

On these types of interest, tax is deducted at 20 per cent from the gross income before handing it over to you. There is no further tax bill if you pay tax at the basic rate on your income – which is the case for the vast majority of taxpayers. If you pay tax at the higher rate, there will be extra tax to pay on this income. If your income is too low to pay tax or the highest rate of tax you pay is the starting rate of 10 per cent only, you can reclaim all or some of the tax which has been deducted.

The savings income is treated as an upper slice of your income. This means the starting rate band is set first against your earnings and other non-savings income (and taxed at 20 per cent).

44 **Tax-saving idea**   If you pay tax at a top rate of 40 or 50 per cent, tax-free investments can be very attractive. Even if you could get a higher advertised rate of return on a taxable investment, the after-tax return could be considerably lower.

45 **Tax-saving idea**   If you have been over-taxed on your savings, claim a refund using form R40. You can go back four years to claim tax back – for example, if you claim by 5 April 2012, you can claim back tax paid as long ago as the 2007–08 tax year.

46 **Tax-saving idea**   If your income is too low to pay tax, you can arrange with the bank or building society to be paid interest without deduction of tax. Fill in form R85 which is available from banks, building societies and post offices, as well as from tax offices and www.hmrc.gov.uk. See www.hmrc.gov.uk/tdsi/key-info.htm for guidance. Once made, the declaration runs indefinitely, so remember to review it if your circumstances change.

47 **Tax-saving idea**   Many people are careful to make the most of their income tax-free allowances each year, but overlook the tax-free capital gains limit. To make regular use of the limit, you could consider selling assets each year and buying them back later or immediately buying similar assets.

48 **Tax-saving idea**   Although there is often no tax for you to pay when you cash in a life insurance policy, the insurance company has already paid tax, which you can't reclaim. Other investments will usually be more tax-efficient. For example, consider unit trusts, investment trusts or open-ended investment companies as alternatives to unit-linked life insurance policies.

Pensions

The government offers tax incentives to encourage you to provide for your retirement by saving with an employer's occupational pension scheme or through your own personal pension or stakeholder scheme. These mean that saving for the future through a pension often provides a better return than any other type of investment:

- there is tax relief on your contributions to the scheme (within limits)
- any employer's contributions made for you are not taxable as your income or as a fringe benefit

- the fund the money goes into pays no capital gains tax and some of the income builds up tax-free
- you can trade in some pension to get a tax-free lump sum when you retire.

49 **Tax-saving idea**   Everyone should try to make sure that they are saving for retirement through a pension – and the earlier you start, the better the pension you should get at the end. You can usually get tax relief at your highest rate of tax. This means a contribution of £1,000 usually costs you just £600 if you are a higher rate tax-payer, and just £800 if you are a basic rate taxpayer. If your income level means you are losing tax credits, a £1,000 pension contribution could increase your credits by up to £410. The effective cost of a £1,000 contribution after tax relief and credits could be reduced to £190 for a higher rate taxpayer and £390 for a basic rate taxpayer.

50 **Tax-saving idea**   Everyone – even a child – can put at least £3,600 a year into a pension scheme. You can make contributions on behalf of someone else – for example, your child or a non-working partner.

51 **Tax-saving idea**   In any one year, you can get tax relief on payments into pension schemes up to 100 per cent of your UK earnings for the year. This may give you scope, for example if you inherit a lump sum, to invest the whole amount tax efficiently for retirement.

52 **Tax-saving idea**   Usually your contributions have to be in money but if you get shares from an employee savings-related share option scheme or share incentive plan you can transfer these tax-free to a pension scheme within 90 days of acquiring them. Future capital growth will then be tax-free and higher rate taxpayers will also pay less tax on any dividends they produce.

53 **Tax-saving idea**   If you are a starting rate taxpayer or non-taxpayer, you still hand over contributions to a per-sonal pension after deducting tax relief at the basic rate. The relief is claimed by the provider from the Revenue and added to your scheme. In this way, you are getting a bonus added to your pension savings. As a non-taxpayer, for every £10 you contribute, the bonus increases your savings by £2.50 in 2011–12.

54 **Tax-saving idea**   Your employer can pay up to £50,000 into a pension scheme for you. This can be particularly useful if you run your own company and so can control how much the employer (the company) pays in. The company gets tax relief on the contributions provided they are 'wholly and exclusively' for the purpose of the business. In practice, this means the contributions must be proportionate to the value of your work.

Options at retirement

55 **Tax-saving idea**   Provided the individual scheme rules allow it, you can take a tax-free lump sum from any type of pension scheme – this includes additional voluntary contribution schemes and all contracted-out schemes.

56 **Tax-saving idea**   If you opt for income withdrawal you do not have to draw any pension at all. You could just take a quarter of your fund as tax-free cash and leave the rest of the fund invested for later.

57 **Tax-saving idea**   If you are getting tax relief on premiums for life cover applied for before 14 December 2006 through a personal pension, be wary of switching to another policy or provider. Premiums for your new policy will not qualify for tax relief and so are likely to cost more overall.

Increasing your state pension

58 **Tax-saving idea**   If you have fewer than 30 qualifying years in your national insurance record, paying voluntary class 3 national insurance contributions could be a good deal. A year's worth of contributions would buy you £177 a year extra state pension, index-linked, and payable from state pension age for the rest of your life.

Individual savings accounts

Individual savings accounts (ISAs) let you invest tax-efficiently in two ways:

- **Cash ISAs**. These are savings accounts with banks, building societies or National Savings & Investments
- **Stocks and shares ISAs**. These are based on stock market investments, such as shares, gilts and corporate bonds or funds investing in these investments (for example, via unit trusts and insurance policies).

Originally, the government had promised that ISAs would be available only until 2010. But now the government has said that they will continue to be available indefinitely.

59 **Tax-saving idea**   Saving through a cash ISA means no tax to pay on your interest. If you would, in any case, save with a bank or building society, make sure you use your ISA allowance each year.

60 **Tax-saving idea**   Higher rate and additional rate tax-payers pay less tax on dividends and similar income earned by investments held in a stocks and shares ISA. This does not apply to other taxpayers – their income is taxed the same whether these investments are held in or outside the ISA. But stocks and shares ISAs investing in gilts and/or corporate bonds produce tax-free income for everyone.

Note that you have to be resident in the UK (unless you are a Crown servant working abroad, or their spouse or civil partner) to put money into an ISA, but if you go abroad after starting one, you don't have to cash it in – it still goes on getting tax relief.

61 **Tax-saving idea** Try to use your ISA allowance each year. Unused allowance can't be carried forward. Once your savings and investments are in an ISA they carry on being sheltered from tax indefinitely and can give you good tax savings. For example, if you had used your full cash ISA allowance every year since ISAs started, you could have built up a fund of over £46,000 by the end of 2010, including tax savings of over £2,000 for a basic rate taxpayer and over £4,000 for a higher rate taxpayer.

62 **Tax-saving idea**   If you give capital to your children and it produces over £100 income a year, that income will normally be taxed as yours. You can avoid this trap by investing in a child trust fund, junior ISA, friendly society tax-efficient plan ('baby bond'), NS&I children's bonus bonds or a stakeholder pension scheme.

7 Making the most of fringe benefits and minimising capital gains tax

Many employers give their employees non-cash fringe benefits as part of their pay package. Typical examples are employer's contributions to a pension scheme, company cars, luncheon vouchers or interest-free loans to buy a season ticket for the railway.

63 **Tax-saving idea** Many fringe benefits are tax-free, and even those which are not can remain good value for employees because the taxable value put on them may be less than it would cost you to pay for the benefit yourself. Try to take advantage of fringe benefits in negotiations with your boss. You do not normally pay national insurance contributions on fringe benefits unless they can be readily converted to cash.

64 **Tax-saving idea** With some fringe benefits, such as pension contributions and childcare vouchers, your employer saves national insurance too and so might be particularly willing to consider a salary sacrifice arrangement. Your contract is amended so you receive less salary but get extra benefits instead. This can be worth doing if you will be better off overall, taking into account the value of the benefits, the tax and national insurance you save and any savings your employer is willing to share with you. But check whether you'll lose out on other pay-related items, such as sick pay.

65 **Tax-saving idea**   If your employer pays mileage allowance at less than the tax-free authorised rates or doesn't
pay any allowance at all, you can claim the shortfall up
to the amount of the authorised rate as an allowable
expense.

66 **Tax-saving idea**   The tax-free authorised mileage rates
will not cover all your costs if you drive a gas-guzzler. You
can save most tax by using a small, fuel-efficient car.

67 **Tax-saving idea**   If you are severely and permanently
disabled and cannot use public transport, financial help
with the cost of travelling to and from work may be available. This could be the loan of a car provided it is adapted
for your use and you are not allowed to make private journeys other than travel between home and work.

68 **Tax-saving idea**   Check carefully whether employer-
provided childcare is a good idea for you. Anything your
employer pays is balanced by a reduction in any working
tax credit childcare element for which you qualify. Bear
in mind that if accepting childcare benefits ultimately
means you are paid less, any pay-related benefits such
as pension savings and life cover would be reduced.

69 **Tax-saving idea** Childcare vouchers from your employer can be used only to pay for approved childcare. This could include, say, a grandparent who gets approval, provided they also look after at least one other unrelated child and the care is not in your own home.

70 **Tax-saving idea** You can receive up to £156 a year tax-free from your employer towards additional household expenses without having to keep records if you have to work from home. Higher amounts can be tax-free but you'll then need records to back up the claim. Additional expenses might include, say, heating, lighting, metered water and business phone calls.

71 **Tax-saving idea** If you can arrange your work so that you count as self-employed rather than an employee, you will be able to claim a much wider range of expenses. But remember there may be disadvantages in not having the protection of employment law.

72 **Tax-saving idea** If you use a car infrequently on business, a pool car from work may be a better option than a company car, since use of a pool car is tax-free. However, the Revenue carefully checks claims to ensure these truly are pool cars. In particular, you should avoid taking a car home overnight.

73 **Tax-saving idea**   From 6 April 2010 to 5 April 2015, a zero-emission company car is a tax-free benefit.

74 **Tax-saving idea**   The taxation of an inefficient company car is onerous. With the tightening of the car scales each year, increasingly this applies to medium-sized as well as large cars. If you are about to get a new car, consider a smaller, more fuel-efficient model.

75 **Tax-saving idea**   Typically both the list price and CO_2 emissions of an automatic are higher than for an equivalent manual car. If your employer provides you with a company car that is an automatic because disability prevents you driving a manual car, the taxable value can be based on the lower emissions for the equivalent manual and you can also use the lower list price.

76 **Tax-saving idea**   If you drive a company car or van in central London, the taxable value of your vehicle already includes any congestion charges (or related penalty charges) that are reimbursed by your employer. There is no need to declare these amounts separately and no further tax to pay on them.

77 **Tax-saving idea** If your employer provides you with a van you take home at night, consider asking your employer to put in writing that you are not allowed to use the van privately. Then, provided any private use is only incidental, the van will be a tax-free benefit. Otherwise, the taxable value of the van and fuel will be £3,500 a year which would mean a yearly tax bill of 20% × £3,500 × £700 if you are a basic rate taxpayer.

78 **Tax-saving idea** Consider asking your employer to provide you with a zero-emission van. For five years from 6 April 2010, there is no tax on this benefit, even if the van is available for your private use.

Minimising capital gains tax

If you own items that increase in value, you may find yourself paying capital gains tax. For example, shares, unit trusts, land, property and antiques can increase in price, giving you a capital gain. If you sell them – or even give them away – you may be faced with a tax bill. The capital gains tax rate was 18 per cent of the chargeable gain from 6 April 2008 up to 22 June 2010, up to 40 per cent in earlier years and up to 28 per cent from 23 June 2010 onwards.

The new 28 per cent rate applying from 23 June 2010 is used on chargeable gains which, when added to your income, push you into the higher rate income tax band. Any charge-able gains falling below the higher rate threshold are taxed at 18 per cent and gains above the threshold are taxed at 28 per cent.

When might tax be due?

You may have to pay this tax whenever you dispose of an asset. What is meant by dispose is not defined by law. But if you sell an asset, swap one asset for another or give something away, this will normally count as a disposal. So will the loss or destruction of an asset (although not if you replace or restore it by claiming on an insurance policy, or by using compensation received).

There are some occasions when there is no capital gains tax to pay, regardless of what is being disposed of or how much it is worth:

- assets passed on when someone dies

- gifts to a husband or wife or between civil partners, unless separated

- gifts to charity and community amateur sports clubs.

Although there are no taxable gains in these circumstances, there are also no losses if the asset is worth less than when you acquired it.

 Tax-saving idea If you are thinking of making a gift to charity of an asset which is showing a loss, think again. You won't be able to claim the loss to reduce other taxable gains (though with gifts of quoted shares or property, you may be able to claim income tax relief). Ideally, find something which is showing a taxable gain to give – there will be no tax to pay on the disposal. Alternatively, sell the asset which is showing a loss and give the proceeds to the charity. That would create an allowable loss which could reduce your tax bill on other disposals.

Tax-free gains

There is no capital gains tax to pay on any gain you make on the following assets:

- your home (though not a second home in most cases)
- private cars
- wasting assets with a useful life of 50 years or less (for example, a boat or caravan)
- personal belongings – known as chattels – sold for less than £6,000
- British money, including sovereigns dated after 1837
- foreign currency for your personal spending abroad (including what you spend on maintaining a home abroad), but not foreign currency accounts
- gains on insurance policies, unless you bought them and were not the original holder, or your wife did so and gave them to you (though you may have to pay part of the insurance company's capital gains tax bill)
- betting, pools or lottery winnings

- National Savings & Investments such as NS&I Certificates and Capital Bonds

- ISAs

- Enterprise Investment Scheme (EIS) shares, provided you have owned them for a minimum period and they carried on their qualifying activity for at least three years

- shares in venture capital trusts

- terminal bonuses on Save-As-You-Earn (SAYE) contracts

- British government stock and any options to buy and sell such stock

- certain corporate bonds such as company loan stock and debentures issued after 13 March 1984 and options to buy and sell such bonds

- interests in trusts or settlements, unless you bought them

- decorations for bravery, unless you bought them

- gifts to certain bodies (such as museums) and gifts of certain heritage property in line with the inheritance tax exemptions

- gifts to charity and to community amateur sports clubs

- damages or compensation for a personal injury or wrong to yourself or in your personal capacity (for example, libel)

- compensation for being given bad investment advice that left you worse off after being persuaded to buy a personal pension between 29 April 1988 and 30 June 1994

- from 6 April 2008 onwards, sale of a business or business assets if you can claim entrepreneurs' relief.

80 **Tax-saving idea** If your spouse or partner is terminally ill, consider giving them any assets you own that are showing large taxable gains, assuming your spouse or partner plans to leave you their estate in their will. There is capital gains tax neither on the transfer to them nor on death. Moreover, you inherit the assets at their market value at the time of death, wiping out the previous gains. Bear in mind that the initial gift will not be accepted as genuine and will not save the intended tax if leaving the assets back to you in the will is a condition of the gift.

81 **Tax-saving idea** If you own a second home, investment property, antiques, collectables or other valuables, keep careful records of what they cost you to buy and maintain. You could face a capital gains tax bill when you dispose of them but allowable expenses can reduce the bill.

82 **Tax-saving idea** The generous treatment of chattels means that collecting can be a very tax-efficient activity. This is especially true if the items in the collection can be sold individually and so taxed separately instead of being treated as a set. This might apply to, say, rare books or unrelated bits of silver.

83 **Tax-saving idea**   Do not forget to claim losses you make when you dispose of, say, shares or valuables. Make sure you claim them within the time limit and keep careful records so that you don't forget them later on.

Capital gains: the tax-free allowance

84 **Tax-saving idea**   Try to use your tax-free allowance every year – you can't carry any unused part over to another year.

85 **Tax-saving idea**   Spouses and civil partners each have a tax-free allowance, so in 2011–12 can have tax-free gains of £21,200 between them. Consider reorganising your possessions and investments (for example, holding them jointly) so that each of you uses up your full allowance before the other starts to pay tax.

86 **Tax-saving idea**   If you accept cash for shares in a takeover, this counts as a disposal for capital gains tax. Sometimes you can opt for loan notes instead. If so, the disposal is deferred until you cash in the loan notes. This is useful if putting off the disposal would reduce the tax you pay (for example, by using a new tax year's allowance).

87 **Tax-saving idea**   Since there is no capital gains tax on gifts between spouses or civil partners, you can effectively double your tax-free band if you are married by giving assets to your spouse to dispose of. So in 2011–12 a married couple can effectively make £21,200 of disposals.

8 Gifts and passing your money on (but not to the tax man)

This chapter tells you how inheritance tax works and how to reduce the amount that goes to the Revenue. It also explains the pre-owned assets tax that came into effect from 6 April 2005 and which does have to be reported on your tax return.

How inheritance tax works

Your chargeable estate

When you die, everything you own – your home, possessions, investments and savings – goes into your estate. So does money paid out by life insurance policies unless they are written in trust, and the value of things you have given away but reserved the right to use for yourself. Debts such as outstanding mortgages and funeral expenses are deducted from the total to find the value of your estate.

Inheritance tax is worked out on a rolling total of gifts you have made over the last seven years. What you leave on death is in effect your final gift.

So, to the estate you leave are added any gifts you made in the seven years before death unless they were tax-free gifts.

Some or all of your estate may be free of inheritance tax: anything left to your spouse or civil partner, or to a UK charity, for example. These tax-free bequests and legacies are deducted from the value of your estate before the tax bill is worked out.

88 **Tax-saving idea**   When the first of a married couple or civil partners dies it may not be clear whether their survivor will need any of their unused tax-free allowance later on. To keep your options open, make sure you keep all the documents relating to the first death.

89 **Tax-saving idea**   You can inherit the unused tax-free allowance from more than one spouse or civil partner who dies before you. But the maximum tax-free allowance you can have is capped at twice the normal personal limit.

Gifts free of inheritance tax

Gifts that are always tax-free:

- gifts between husband and wife or civil partners – even if the two are legally separated. But only the first £55,000 is tax-free if the gifts are to someone who is not domiciled in the UK (domicile reflects the individual's natural home, see Chapter 9)
- gifts to UK charities and community amateur sports clubs
- gifts to certain national institutions such as the National Trust, National Gallery, British Museum (and their Scottish, Welsh and Northern Ireland equivalents)

- gifts of certain types of heritage property such as paintings, archives, land or historic buildings to non-profit-making concerns like local museums

- gifts of land in the UK to registered housing associations

- gifts of shares in a company into a trust for the benefit of most or all of the employees which will control the company

- gifts to established political parties.

Gifts that are tax-free on death only:

- lump sums paid out on your death by a pension scheme provided the trustees of the scheme have discretion about who gets the money

- refunds of personal pension contributions (and interest) paid directly to someone else or a trust – in other words, not paid into your estate

- the estate of anyone killed on active military service in war or whose death was hastened by such service

- £10,000 *ex gratia* payments received by survivors (and their spouses) held as Japanese prisoners of war during World War Two and amounts from other specified schemes that also provide compensation for wrongs suffered during the war.

Gifts that are tax-free in lifetime only:

- anything given to an individual more than seven years before your death – unless there are strings attached

- small gifts worth up to £250 to any number of people in any tax year. But you can't give anyone more than this limit and claim exemption on the first £250 – if you give someone £500, the whole £500 will be taxable unless it is tax-free for one of the other reasons below

- regular gifts that are treated as normal expenditure out of income. The gifts must come out of your after-tax income and not from your capital. After paying for the gifts, you should have enough income to maintain your normal standard of living

- gifts on marriage to a bride or groom or on registration to civil partners: each parent of the bride, groom or partner can give £5,000, grandparents or remoter relatives and the bride, groom or partners themselves can give £2,500 and anyone else £1,000. The gifts must be made before the big day – and if the marriage or registration is called off, the gift becomes taxable

- gifts for the maintenance of your family – your current or a former husband, wife or civil partner, certain dependent relatives and children under 18 or still in full-time education. The children can be yours, stepchildren, adopted children or any other children in your care

- up to £3,000 in total a year of other gifts. If you don't use the whole £3,000 annual exemption in one year, you can carry forward the unused part to the next tax year only. You can't use the annual exemption to top up the small gifts exemption. If you give someone more than £250 in a year, all of it must come off the annual exemption if it is to be free of inheritance tax.

Planning for inheritance tax

90 **Tax-saving idea**   Draw up a will. There are simple steps you can take to minimise the tax payable on your estate when you die and to reduce the complications for those you leave behind.

91 **Tax-saving idea**   Make as full use as possible of the lifetime gifts you can make which do not fall into the inheritance tax net, such as those which count as normal expenditure from income or fall within the £3,000 annual allowance.

92 **Tax-saving idea**   Share your wealth with your spouse or civil partner so that you can each make tax-free lifetime gifts and efficient wills. There is no inheritance tax or capital gains tax on gifts between spouses or civil partners.

93 **Tax-saving idea**   Use life insurance to blunt the impact of inheritance tax. Policies written in trust go straight to the beneficiary and don't form part of your estate. Premiums you pay are tax-free gifts if they count as normal expenditure out of income or fall within the £3,000 a year exemption.

94 **Tax-saving idea** Consider estate freezing by, for example, paying premiums to an investment-type life insurance policy written in trust for the person to whom you wish to make the gift. They get any growth in the value of the investment instead of it counting as part of your estate.

95 **Tax-saving idea** A deed of variation can be used to alter the way an estate is shared out. This could save tax on a subsequent death.

9 How to save money when filling in your tax return

The Revenue has been trying to reduce the number of people who have to fill in the full tax return. If you get most of your income through the PAYE system, you may just be sent a PAYE review form. If your affairs are fairly straight-forward, you may be sent a short tax return of four pages and no supplements.

If your affairs are more complex, you will be sent the full tax return. It is also up to you to request the full return if the review form or short return is not suitable given your circumstances.

96 **Tax-saving idea**   Avoid simple mistakes that could cause your tax return to be rejected and possibly cause a £100 late-filing penalty. Common errors include: ticking yes to questions but failing to send the supplementary pages, sending information on a separate sheet instead of on the tax return itself, writing notes such as 'per accounts' or 'information to follow' instead of putting in figures (albeit provisional ones), and failing to sign and date the return.

Income

The first stage in working out your income tax bill is to find your taxable income. The Main tax return asks about the most common types of income, such as interest from savings accounts, pensions and some state benefits. If you have any more unusual types of income, such as interest from gilts or gains from life insurance policies, you will need to complete the Additional information form.

97 **Tax-saving idea**   Take advantage of the ways you can save which are free of tax: pension schemes, some ISAs and some National Savings & Investment (NS&I) products. These are especially helpful if you are a higher rate taxpayer. If you are a basic rate taxpayer, check to see that any expenses, for example for managing an ISA, are not more than the tax saved.

98 **Tax-saving idea**   Couples, where one person pays tax at a higher rate than the other, can adjust their investments between them, so that more investments are in the name of the lower taxpayer. Thus less of the return will be taxed at the higher rates. Couples, where one pays tax at the starting rate or pays no tax at all and the other pays at the basic rate, can save tax in the same way by shifting interest-earning investments (but not shares or unit trusts) to the lower taxpayer.

99 **Tax-saving idea**   Compensation paid by UK banks to Holocaust victims or their heirs has been tax-free since 8 May 2000. This exemption has been backdated to 1996–

97 and applies to similar compensation paid by foreign banks. If you have paid tax on such a payment in the past, you should send an amended tax return to your tax office in order to claim the tax back – the normal time limit for amending returns does not apply.

Pensions and benefits that should not be included in your tax return

If you received any of the following, you do not need to give details here in the tax return because they are tax-free:

- attendance allowance, disability living allowance, severe disablement allowance, including age-related addition
- bereavement payment
- council tax benefit, housing benefit (rent rebates and allowances), home renovation and repair grants
- educational maintenance allowance
- Employment Zone payments
- guardian's allowance
- income-related employment and support allowance (and incapacity benefit if it replaced invalidity benefit that you were receiving before 13 April 1995 and there has been no break in your claim; otherwise incapacity benefit is taxable)
- income support (if you're not required to be available for work)

- industrial injuries benefit (except death benefit)
- jobfinder's grant, employment training and employment rehabilitation allowances, back-to-work bonus and New Deal training allowances
- maternity allowance, child benefit, child tax credit, additions to benefits or state pensions because you have a dependent child, school uniform grants and fares to school
- pension credit and pensioners' Christmas bonus
- pensions and benefits for wounds or disability in military service or for other war injuries, war widow's pension and some similar pensions for dependants
- social fund payments
- student grants, bursaries, scholarships and loans
- vaccine damage payments
- winter fuel payments and cold weather payments
- working tax credit
- similar benefits to those above paid by foreign governments.

Pensions and benefits that should be entered in your tax return

Details of the following should be entered here:

- additions to benefits or state pensions for an adult dependant

- carer's allowance
- contribution-based employment and support allowance, incapacity benefit
- income withdrawals from a personal pension plan where the purchase of an annuity has been deferred
- industrial death benefit pension (but not child allowance), pension for injuries at work or for work-related illnesses
- Jobseeker's Allowance (up to the taxable amount)
- pension from a former employer or a pension from your late husband or wife's employer, pension from a free-standing additional voluntary contribution, pension from service in the armed forces
- pension from a personal pension scheme or retirement annuity contract or trust scheme
- state retirement pension, including the basic pension, state additional pension and graduated pension and lump sum from deferring state pension
- statutory sick pay, statutory maternity pay, statutory paternity pay and statutory adoption pay paid by the Revenue
- widowed mother's allowance and widowed parent's allowance, widow's pension and bereavement pension.

100 **Tax-saving idea** Taking a lump sum as a result of deferring your state pension will not push you into a higher tax bracket. The whole lump sum is taxed at the highest rate you were paying without the lump sum (ignoring the special rate that applies to savings income and dividends).

22 **Tax-saving idea** If you are a basic rate taxpayer and your only untaxed income each year is interest from gilts, it could be worth opting to receive interest from gilts with tax already deducted. That way, you may not need to fill in a tax return in future.

Tax reliefs

You can pay less tax by spending more money on things the government wants to encourage – and thus gives tax relief on – such as pensions and gifts to charity. In some instances you can get tax relief at your highest rate of tax, which could be 50 per cent. Assuming that you want to spend the money, buying any of these things could be highly advantageous.

You get your tax relief in different ways. Frequently you get basic rate tax relief by deducting it from what you spend. Any higher rate tax relief that is due you will claim in your tax return and give yourself the relief when you are working out your tax bill. Or you could get higher rate relief through your PAYE code. Non-taxpayers will not have to repay the tax deducted, except in the case of Gift Aid.

102 **Tax-saving idea**   Nearly everyone can pay up to £3,600 a year into a pension scheme. In 2010–11 and 2011–12 this works out at £2,880 a year after deducting the basic rate tax relief. You get the relief even if you are a non-taxpayer or pay tax only at the starting rate.

103 **Tax-saving idea**   You cannot ask for pension contributions paid in one tax year to be treated as if they were paid in the previous year. Therefore, you may need to plan carefully to maximise tax relief on your pension contributions. Be prepared to vary them from year to year so that you pay more in years when your taxable income is higher.

104 **Tax-saving idea**   Provided you are a taxpayer, try to arrange gifts to charity through the Gift Aid scheme. The charity you support can receive more by reclaiming basic rate tax relief on what you give. If you are a couple, make sure the donation is made by whichever one of you has the highest rate of tax.

105 **Tax-saving idea**   If your income is over £150,000, your top rate of tax is 50 per cent and this is the rate of relief you will get on Gift Aid donations, making your gifts to charity particularly tax-efficient.

06 **Tax-saving idea** If a charity you want to give to runs a retail Gift Aid scheme this could be a convenient, as well as tax-efficient, way of donating the proceeds from selling a valuable possession, such as a painting, jewellery, antique furniture or other collectors' item. Provided the exemption for personal belongings – chattels – applies, there will be no capital gains tax and you'll get Gift Aid relief on the donation. You cannot get tax relief on any commission the charity charges for selling the item.

07 **Tax-saving idea** Gift Aid declarations are often indefinite, covering any future donations you make to the charity concerned as well as your current gift. Be careful to stop any open-ended declarations if your circumstances change and you are no longer a taxpayer or if you want to make an unusually large gift (out of an inheritance, say) which will not be matched by your tax bill. Otherwise you will find the Revenue billing you for tax relief that the charity claims.

08 **Tax-saving idea** If you want to make a substantial gift to charity and you own shares or property which are standing at a substantial profit, it will usually be more tax-efficient to give the shares or property direct to the charity rather than selling them first and making a Gift Aid donation of the cash raised. But the tax relief you get can only be set against your income – not any capital gains.

Allowances

Another legal way of reducing the amount of income tax you have to pay is to claim any allowances to which you are entitled. These are deducted from your income, along with reliefs (deductions), to make your taxable income smaller – and so also your tax bill.

Personal allowances

Most people get a personal allowance (which is, however, reduced if your income exceeds £100,000 in 2010–11 and disappears altogether when your income exceeds £112,950). You get any personal allowance automatically – you don't have to claim it in your tax return.

109 **Tax-saving idea** You can go back four years to claim allowances that you forgot to claim at the time or didn't know you were entitled to. You will get tax relief at the rate you should have got it had you claimed the allowance at the right time. Provided you claim by 5 April 2013, you can go back as far as the 2008–09 tax year.

Employment, share schemes and self-employment

Employment basics

⓪ **Tax-saving idea** A disadvantage of being an employee is that you cannot deduct as many expenses from your taxable income as you could if you were self-employed. So if you are setting up on your own, check that you will meet the Revenue's conditions for self-employment.

What is taxed

⑪ **Tax-saving idea** You must pay income tax and national insurance on any deemed payment for the tax year in which the money is earned by your personal service company. If that money is paid out to you as salary in a later year, tax and national insurance will again be due – in other words, the same income will be taxed twice. To avoid this, make sure any deemed payment retained within the company is eventually paid out as dividends, not salary. IR35 rules allow dividends up to the amount of any deemed payments to be paid without further tax being due and dividends are not in any case subject to national insurance.

112 **Tax-saving idea**   If you have a choice, consider a zero-emission company van. In that case, the taxable value of fuel for private use of a company van is zero. And, from 6 April 2010 to 5 April 2015, the taxable value of a zero-emission van available for your private use is reduced to zero.

113 **Tax-saving idea**   The taxable value of a company car is based on its carbon dioxide emissions. This makes larger company cars an expensive fringe benefit. Consider a low-emission car instead. You can find out about different cars' carbon dioxide emissions from www.vcacarfuel data.org.uk.

You should ask for and keep receipts for the subsistence and other business expenses you incur to back up your claim.

The rules can be interpreted in a number of ways depending on the facts of the case. If you are unsure what you can claim, the Revenue guide 490: *Employee travel – a tax and NICs guide for employers* (to which your employer should have access and which is available from the Revenue website www.hmrc.gov.uk/helpsheets/490.htm) gives the full rules and useful examples.

Add together all the allowable travel costs incurred, including accommodation and meal costs on business journeys and any other expenses of business journeys (such as business phone calls, but not personal items like phone calls home).

14 **Tax-saving idea**   If you travel for work and it counts as business travel, don't forget to include the cost of any meals and accommodation which are attributable to the journey (other than the usual expenses you incur when at your normal place of work).

15 **Tax-saving idea**   Revenue-agreed flat-rate expenses were increased from the start of 2008–09 (having been unchanged since 2004–05). Make sure you are claiming the increased amount. If your actual expenses come to more than the flat rate, you can claim your actual expenses instead.

16 **Tax-saving idea**   Working from home could mean part being classified as business premises and so trigger a charge for business rates. But, in a case during 2003 , a tribunal ruled that, where home-based working used furniture and equipment normally found in a home, there was no breach of residential use and business rates were not due. However, structural alterations, hiring staff, using specialist equipment and customers visiting your home-business could justify business rates.

17 **Tax-saving idea**   The rules concerning working from home are less strict where your employer reimburses you for certain costs you incur. Since 6 April 2003, where you regularly work from home with your employer's agreement, you can receive up to £3 a week tax-free from your employer towards extra day-to-day costs of running part of your home as an office. Neither you nor your employer has to keep any records to back up these payments and there is no requirement to prove that working from home is a necessary feature of the job.

Share schemes

Part of your payment from a job may come in the form of shares (or share options – the right to buy shares at a set price at some point in the future) in your employer's company. Generally pay in the form of shares is taxable just as any other form of pay or benefit would be. However, there are special approved schemes under which you can get your shares or options tax-free.

118 **Tax-saving idea**   Each year you have an allowance that lets you make some capital gains tax-free (£10,100 in 2010–11). Try to choose the timing of selling your shares to keep your gains within the tax-free limit.

Different types of share schemes

For tax purposes, share schemes fall within five broad categories:

- approved profit-sharing schemes
- approved share incentive plan
- approved share option schemes – either savings-related schemes, company share option schemes or enterprise management incentive options
- unapproved share option schemes
- cheap or free gifts of shares through an unapproved scheme (sometimes called share incentive schemes).

9 **Tax-saving idea** As an employee, you do not often have a choice of a share save scheme, since employers are likely either to have just one scheme, or to have one scheme that is open to all employees and another which is open to a select few. But if you know that your employer is considering a scheme, try to make your voice heard so that the choice suits you.

120 Tax-saving idea   When you take your shares out of an approved profit-sharing scheme, savings-related share option scheme or approved share incentive plan, you can transfer them into an ISA, providing you do so within 90 days. Alternatively, shares from any of these schemes may be transferred within 90 days to a pension scheme. In both cases, the transfer does not trigger a capital gains tax bill at the time and any future growth in the value of the shares is free of capital gains tax.

121 Tax-saving idea   Persuade your employer to set up a share incentive plan. Your employer can give you up to £6,000 of shares a year tax-free as long as you keep them in the scheme for five years.

122 Tax-saving idea   If you are granted options in an approved share option scheme, keep records of when you exercise them, and the dates by which you can next do so. For example, if you were granted options in 2002, you must exercise them by 2012 to avoid tax.

123 Tax-saving idea   Whether or not you will benefit from a savings-related share option scheme depends on the option price and the share price when you exercise your option. You do not have to exercise your option if you would make a loss (in other words, the market price has fallen below the option exercise price). You can instead simply take the tax-free cash. So, especially if you are a higher rate taxpayer, or are optimistic that you will make some profit on the shares, joining the scheme is worthwhile.

Self-employment

Are you self-employed?

Self-employed people are able to claim more income tax reliefs than employed people and they usually pay less in national insurance, so you may need to prove to your tax office that you really are self-employed. Ask yourself the following questions:

- Do you control how your business is run? For example, do you decide what work you take on, where you do the work, what hours you keep?

- Is your own money at risk in the business? For example, have you had to pay for your own premises, do you have to finance the lag between incurring costs and receiving payments?

- Do you have to meet any losses as well as keeping any profits?

- Do you provide the major equipment necessary for your work – for example computer and photocopier for office-based work or machinery for an engineering business? It's not enough that you provide your own small tools – many employees do this too.

- Are you free to employ other people to help you fulfil the contracts you take on? Do you pay your employees yourself?

- If a job doesn't come up to scratch, do you have to redo it or correct it in your own time and at your expense?

The more of these questions to which you can answer 'yes', the more likely it is that you are self-employed. And if you answer 'yes' to all of them, you generally will count as self-employed. But it is the whole picture and facts of your case that determine your work status. Sometimes the decision is not clear cut – for example, if you are newly in business doing work for just one client, perhaps working at a former employer's premises on a freelance basis. Beware if you work through an agency – for example as an agency carer or temporary secretary. Even if you choose whether or not to take on a particular job, you will almost certainly count as an employee rather than self-employed.

124 **Tax-saving idea** As a self-employed person, you can claim more tax reliefs than an employee. Nonetheless, small businesses can still usually save income tax and national insurance by operating as a company provided they are judged to be genuinely in business on their own account (rather than as a device for disguising employee status).

125 **Tax-saving idea** If you take up fostering children, your receipts are tax-free up to a qualifying amount. In 2010–11, this amount is £10,000 a year per household. In addition, each foster carer can claim £200 a week for each child under 11 and £250 a week for each child aged 11 or more. Private fostering arrangements are not eligible for this scheme.

26 **Tax-saving idea**   If you are self-employed and your annual turnover is less than £73,000 from 1 April 2011, you can choose whether or not to register for VAT. Being registered means you can reclaim VAT on things you buy for your business, but you must also charge your customers VAT on your whole turnover (not just the bit in excess of £73,000).

27 **Tax-saving idea**   Since 1 April 2009, the Revenue can visit your business premises, either at any reasonable time or on seven days' notice, for the purpose of checking your tax position. You can be asked to produce virtually any information and documents relating to your past, present or future tax liabilities. If your record-keeping is haphazard, this may trigger a Revenue investigation into your affairs. To lessen the chance of an enquiry and the disruption and expense it can entail, make sure that you keep proper records for your business and that they are more or less up to date at all times.

128 **Tax-saving idea** Claim all the allowable expenses you can. If you're not sure whether an expense is allowable, deduct it from your taxable profits but ask your tax office to confirm whether this is correct.

129 **Tax-saving idea** Be wary of using part of your home exclusively for business – there may be capital gains tax on part of the proceeds when you come to sell your home. Ensuring some private use of your work space – for example, for private study, hobbies, civic duties or other voluntary work – reduces the proportion of home-related expenses you can claim as business expenses, but you should escape capital gains tax.

130 **Tax-saving idea** If you employ a family member in your business, there is no income tax or national insurance on their earnings if you pay them less than the 'primary threshold' (£7,228 in 2011–12). But consider paying them at least the 'lower earnings limit' (£5,304 in 2011–12), so they build up an entitlement to certain state benefits, such as state retirement pension.

131 **Tax-saving idea** In 2011–12, you can get extra tax relief on capital spending over £100,000 if the extra spending is on items that are environmentally friendly and qualify for 100 per cent first-year capital allowances.

32 **Tax-saving idea**   At £2.50 a week, class 2 national insurance contributions are a good value way of building up rights to state benefits such as state basic pension. If your profits are low, think carefully before deciding not to pay these contributions. However, people reaching state pension age on or after 6 April 2010 need only 30 years' worth of contributions to qualify for the full state basic pension. If you already have 30 years' contributions, you get less value from continuing to pay class 2 contributions.

33 **Tax-saving idea**   If you are an employer in business and prefer to avoid the administration involved in operating PAYE, consider contracting a payroll bureau or accountant to do the job for you. The fees you pay can be deducted as expenses of your business.

UK property and being non-resident

If you take in lodgers in your home, providing meals and other services, this may amount to a form of business.

134 **Tax-saving idea** Where you own a rental property with your spouse or civil partner, you must split the taxable income between you in the same shares as you own the property (usually equal shares unless you have made a declaration specifying some other split). But if you own property jointly with anyone else, you can agree to divide the income in different shares from those in which you own the property provided the actual shares you receive are the same as those agreed. For example, an unmarried couple who pay tax at different rates can agree to have more of the rent paid to the lower taxpayer.

The Rent a Room scheme

The Rent a Room scheme applies to rent from letting out furnished accommodation in your home and income from providing any related services, such as providing meals or doing your lodger's laundry. In the normal way you would pay tax on any profit you make – in other words, the income you get less allowable expenses you incur. If instead you opt for the Rent a Room scheme, the first slice of the income is tax-free, but you are not allowed to deduct any expenses.

135 **Tax-saving idea** If you make a profit from taking in lodgers and your income from the lettings is £4,250 or less, there will be no tax to pay on this income if you opt for the Rent a Room scheme. If your gross income from the lettings is more than £4,250 but the expenses and allowances you can claim come to £4,250 or less, you will pay less tax if you opt for the Rent a Room scheme. Using the Rent a Room scheme can save you administration because, for tax purposes, you need only keep records of your income, not any expenses.

36 **Tax-saving idea**   The Revenue accepts that work which once counted as an improvement to a property may over time and due to technological advances now be accepted as a repair and so count as an allowable expense. The example it gives is replacing old windows with double glazing. If you are replacing an old feature with a modern equivalent, try claiming and ask your tax office to confirm that the expense is allowable.

Non-residence

If you are a resident of the UK, you are usually liable for UK tax on all your income whether it comes from within the UK or abroad. But, if you count as a non-resident, there is no UK tax on your income from abroad, only on any income which originates in the UK.

You are likely to be non-resident (or non-domicile) if:

- you are normally a UK resident but you are working abroad for an extended period

- you have been a UK resident but you are going to live abroad permanently or indefinitely – for example because you are retiring abroad

- you have been resident elsewhere but you are based in the UK for now or you have returned for permanent residence.

137 **Tax-saving idea** If you are a long-term UK resident but not UK domiciled (for example, you have married and settled in the UK but still consider another country to be your permanent home), from 2008–09 onwards you may have to choose between:

- paying UK tax each year on your foreign income and gains as they arise whether or not you bring the income and gains into the UK, or

- paying no UK tax on your foreign income and gains but losing your personal allowance (worth up to £2,990 to a higher rate taxpayer in tax savings); losing your capital gains tax allowance (worth up to £1,818 in tax savings); and paying an extra tax bill of £30,000.

Choose the option which results in the lower tax bill. You can choose a different option each year and this may be worth doing if your foreign income and gains vary a lot or you have a big gain in one year only (say, from the sale of a property abroad). Members of a couple each make their own choice – they do not have to be the same.

38 **Tax-saving idea**   If you go to work or live abroad, make sure your trips back home average less than 91 days a year and come to less than 183 days in any single tax year to avoid paying UK taxes on your overseas income.

39 **Tax-saving idea**   Taking a long lease of three years on a home abroad would help to show that you intended to live abroad permanently.

10 Useful leaflets, forms and contacts

You can get these leaflets from any tax office (look in the phone book under HM Revenue & Customs).

Most are also available from www.hmrc.gov.uk or by calling 08459 000 404.

Increasingly, the Revenue is ceasing to publish printed leaflets and instead putting information on its website where it can easily be kept up to date. If you do not have access to the internet, phone the helplines listed in this Appendix and ask to be sent a print-out of the information on the website.

Introduction to self-assessment

RK BK1   Self-assessment. A general guide to keeping records

General guides to the Revenue

Tax appeals

IR160   Enquiries under self-assessment
AO1   The Adjudicator's Office for complaints
C/FS   Complaints and putting things right
COP10   Information and advice (online only)

Income tax for particular groups

IR121   Approaching retirement – a guide to tax and national insurance contributions
Pensioners – www.hmrc.gov.uk/pensioners/approaching.htm

Pride1   Taxes and benefits – information for our lesbian, gay, bisexual and transgender customers

CA5603   To pay voluntary national insurance contributions

Tax credits

WTC1   Child tax credit and working tax credit. An introduction

WTC5   Help with the cost of childcare

WTC8   Child tax credit and working tax credit (overpayments)

WTC10   Tax credits. Help us to help you get it right

WTC/AP   Child tax credit and working tax credit: how to appeal against a tax credit decision or award

(no ref.) Tax credits: how HMRC handle exit credit overpayments

COP26   What happens if we have paid you too much tax credit?

WTC/FS1 Tax credits enquiry

Income tax and international issues

HMRC6   Residence, domicile and the remittance basis

Savings and investments

IR111   Bank and building society interest. Are you paying tax when you don't need to?

(no ref.) ISA factsheet

Employees

480   Expenses and benefits. A tax guide

IR115   Paying for childcare. Getting help from your employer

IR177   Share incentive plans and your entitlement to benefits

Self-employed

SE1   Are you thinking of working for yourself?

ES/FS1   Employed or self-employed for tax and national insurance contributions

CA72B   Deferring self-employed national insurance contributions

Employers (also see *Employees* above)

490   Employee travel. A tax and NICs guide for employers

P11DX   How to cut down on your paperwork: dispensations

Capital gains tax

www.hmrc.gov.uk/cgt

Inheritance tax

HM Revenue & Customs no longer publishes any leaflets about inheritance tax. Instead see its customer guide to inheritance tax at www.hmrc.gov.uk/inheritancetax.

Inheritance tax is not dealt with by your usual tax office. Instead contact HMRC Inheritance Tax at:

England and Wales: Ferrers House, PO Box 38, Castle Meadow Road, Nottingham, NG2 1BB

Scotland: Meldrum House, 15 Drumsheugh Gardens, Edinburgh EH3 7UG

Northern Ireland: Level 5, Millennium House, 17–25 Great Victoria Street, Belfast BT2 7BN

Probate and Inheritance Tax Helpline: 0845 302 0900

Revenue background notes on businesses

The Revenue publishes Business Economic Notes (BENs) on its website at www.hmrc.gov.uk/bens but these are very out of date. The Revenue had started to publish more recent Tactical and Information Packages (TIPs) but, following a review of its publications policy, decided to withdraw them. If you are the subject of an enquiry, ask the officer dealing with your case whether they are drawing on information from a TIP and, if so, ask for a copy.

Useful Revenue forms

You can get these forms from tax offices, the Revenue website www.hmrc.gov.uk (follow the link to 'Find a form') or by calling 0845 900 0404.

CWF1	To register if you are newly self-employed
IHT100	To report a taxable lifetime gift for inheritance tax*
IHT205	Simplified return of estate where no inheritance tax due*
IHT400	Inheritance tax account*
P11D	Summary of your taxable fringe benefits (from your employer)
P2	Notice of coding**
P38(S)	For students working in holidays who want to be paid gross
P50	Claiming tax back when you have stopped working
P60	End of year certificate of PAYE deductions (from your employer)
P86	To determine residence and domicile issues
P810	Tax review form if you pay tax through PAYE**
R40	To claim a tax repayment
R85	To register to receive savings interest gross
SA100	The full tax return (main form). You may need supplements as well
SA200	Short tax return (not available from website)**
SA300	Self assessment statement if you pay tax under self assessment**

SA303   To claim to reduce payments on account

VAT1   To register for VAT

* From website or Probate and Inheritance Tax Helpline 0845 302 0900.

** Your tax office sends you this form if relevant to you.

Revenue helplines

Here are a few examples. For a full list visit www.hmrc.gov. uk and click on 'Contact us' at the top of the screen.

Helpline for Newly Self-Employed: 0845 915 4515

Individual Savings Accounts Helpline: 0845 604 1701

National insurance enquiries: 0845 302 1479

New Employer Helpline (NESI): 0845 60 70 143

Probate and Inheritance Tax Helpline: 0845 302 0900

Self Assessment Helpline: 0845 900 0444

Self Assessment Forms Orderline: 0845 900 0404

Taxation of bank and building society interest: 0845 980 0645

Tax Credits: 0845 300 3900

VAT Helpline: 0845 010 9000

Advice about tax

Chartered Institute of Taxation
First Floor, 11–19 Artillery Row, London SW1P 1RT
Tel: 020 7340 0550/0844 579 6700
www.tax.org.uk
For list of members who give professional tax advice for a fee

TaxAid
Room 304, Linton House, 164–180 Union Street, London SE1 0LH
Tel: 0845 120 3779
www.taxaid.org.uk
Free tax help for people on a low income

Tax Help for Older People (TOP)
Pineapple Business Park, Salway Ash, Bridport, Dorset DT6 5DB
Tel: 0845 601 3321/01308 488 066
www.taxvol.org.uk
Free tax help for older people on a low income

140 **Tax-saving idea** Whenever you contact HM Revenue & Customs, make sure you make a note of the conversation for your records in case of dispute later on.

European Economic Area (EEA) countries

Austria
Belgium
Bulgaria (since January 2007)
Cyprus (since May 2004)
Czech Republic (since May 2004)
Denmark
Estonia (since May 2004)
Finland
France
Germany
Greece
Hungary (since May 2004)
Iceland
Ireland
Italy

Latvia (since May 2004)
Liechtenstein
Lithuania (since May 2004)
Luxembourg
Malta (since May 2004)
Netherlands
Norway
Poland (since May 2004)
Portugal
Romania (since January 2007)
Slovakia (since May 2004)
Slovenia (since May 2004)
Spain
Sweden
United Kingdom

Index

allowances 2, 7, 54
  capital 114
  capital gains 85–6
  married couple 52
  personal 52, 104
  transfer of 52–3

benefits 11–13
  tax returns and 99–100
bereavement 56
Business Economic Notes (BEN)
        125
Business Payment Support
        Service 33

capital gains tax 9, 19, 27, 55, 124
  inheritance 63
  lettings 63
  main home 61
  property 59–63
  shares 108
  tax-free allowance 85–6
  tax-free gains 82–3
certificates of tax deposit 31
child tax credit 13, 58, 123
child trust fund (CTF) 13
childcare vouchers 76, 78
children/young people 69
  childcare costs 58
  gifts to 57, 73
  tax system and 56–7
company car/van 78–80, 106

determination 25–6

fostering 112–13
fringe benefits (employee)
        76–80, 124

Gift Aid donations 7, 96, 101–3
gifts 89–91
  see also inheritance tax

HM Revenue & Customs 18, 40
  discovery assessments 42–3
  enquiries 41–2
  First-Tier Tribunal 42
  forms 126–7
  helplines 127
  interventions 41
  leaflets/information 122–5
  tax calculation 26–7
  website 24–5
Holocaust victims 97–8
home, use for business purposes
        59, 62, 108

income 2, 4–5, 97
  investment income 13, 66–8
  tax-free 5, 10–11, 14–15
income tax x, 1–7, 27, 96, 123
  bands 3
  see also PAYE, self-assessment
individual savings accounts (ISAs)
        1, 57, 58, 66, 72–3, 97, 110

cash 72
  factsheet 123
  stocks and shares 72
inheritance tax 55, 63, 88–93, 125
  chargeable estate 88–9
  life insurance and 92
  planning for 92–3
investments 66–8, 97, 123

jointly owned assets 51

lettings 59, 63, 115–17
  see also Rent a Room scheme

maintenance payments 14, 54
marriage/civil partnerships 50–3
  living together 56
  separation/divorce 53–5
  tax allowances 97
  see also maintenance payments

national insurance contributions
    (NICs) 33, 54, 115
National Savings & Investment
    (NS&I) Certificates 13, 66,
    97
non domicile 117

PAYE (Pay As You Earn) 18–19,
    27–8, 33–7, 96
  claiming a tax refund 35
  coding notice 34–5
  students and 36–7
pensions 11–12, 68–71, 76
  occupational 68
  personal/stakeholder 68
  state 7, 54, 71, 100
  tax returns and 98, 100
private residence relief 59–61

reliefs, tax 2, 6, 101–3
  self-employment 112
Rent a Room scheme 14, 117–18
retirement 71, 122
  see also pensions

Save-As-You-Earn (SAYE)
    schemes 13
self-assessment 18, 27, 29, 30,
    45, 122
self-employment 111–15, 124
share schemes 108–10
students 36–7, 57

tax credits 56, 123
tax returns 21–2, 95–119
  appeals 47–8, 122
  changes to 40–5
  common errors 96
  deadlines 22–3, 47
  expenses 106, 114, 124
  filing by internet 24
  information checks 43–4
  interest charges/surcharges
    30–1
  non-residence 117–19
  payments 27–8, 29–33
  penalties 20, 25–6, 45–6
  premises costs 107
  record-keeping 19–21, 44–5
  travel costs 107
  see also HM Revenue & Customs

VAT 113

wills 92
working tax credit 3, 13